Early Letters
of
George Wm. Curtis
to
John S. Dwight

KENNIKAT PRESS SCHOLARLY REPRINTS

Dr. Ralph Adams Brown, Senior Editor

Series on

LITERARY AMERICA IN THE NINETEENTH CENTURY

Under the General Editorial Supervision of
Dr. Walter Harding
University Professor, State University of New York

Early Letters
of
George Wm. Curtis
to
John S. Dwight
Brook Farm and Concord
Edited by
George Willis Cooke

KENNIKAT PRESS
Port Washington, N. Y./London

EARLY LETTERS OF GEORGE WM. CURTIS TO JOHN S. DWIGHT

First published in 1898
Reissued in 1971 by Kennikat Press
Library of Congress Catalog Card No: 72-122647
ISBN 0-8046-1295-1

Manufactured by Taylor Publishing Company   Dallas, Texas

CONTENTS

———

EARLY LIFE AT BROOK FARM
AND CONCORD

EARLY LIFE AT BROOK FARM
AND CONCORD

GEORGE WILLIAM CURTIS was born in Providence, February 24, 1824. From the age of six to eleven he was in the school of C. W. Greene at Jamaica Plain, and then, until he was fifteen, attended school in Providence. His brother Burrill, two years older, was his inseparable companion, and they were strongly attached to each other. About 1835 Curtis came under the influence of Ralph Waldo Emerson, who was heard by him in Providence, and who commanded his boyish admiration. Burrill Curtis has said of this interest of himself and his brother that it proved to be the cardinal event of their youth; and what this experience was he has described.

"I still recall," he says, "the impressions produced by Emerson's delivery of his address on 'The Over-Soul' in Mr. Hartshorn's school-room in Providence. He seemed to speak as an inhabitant of heaven, and with the inspiration and

A   1

authority of a prophet. Although a large part
of the matter of that discourse, when reduced
to its lowest terms, does not greatly differ from
the commonplaces of piety and religion, yet its
form and its tone were so fresh and vivid that
they made the matter also seem to be uttered
for the first time, and to be a direct outcome
from the inmost source of the highest truth.
We heard Emerson lecture frequently, and made
his personal acquaintance. My enthusiastic admiration of him and his writings soon mounted
to a high and intense hero-worship, which, when
it subsided, seems to have left me ever since in-
capable of attaching myself as a follower to any
other man. How far George shared such feelings, if at all, I cannot precisely say; but he so
far shared my enthusiastic admiration as to be
led a willing captive to Emerson's attractions,
and to the incidental attractions of the movement of which he was the head; and Emerson
always continued to command from us both the
sincerest reverence and homage."

Burrill went so far as to discontinue the use
of money and animal food; both the brothers
discarded the conventional costumes in matters
of dress, and their interest was enlisted in the reforms of the day. The family removed to New
York in 1839, George studied at home with tu-
tors, and was an attendant at the church of Dr.
Orville Dewey.

I

THE warm and active interest of the brothers in the Transcendental movement, in all its phases, led them to propose to their father that he permit them to attend the school connected with the Brook Farm Association. Permission having been granted, they became boarders there in the spring or summer of 1842. At no time were they members of the association, and they paid for their board and tuition as they would have done at any seminary or college.

At this time the Brook Farm Association had two sources of income—the farm of about two hundred acres, and the school which was carried on in connection therewith. In fact, the school was more largely profitable than the farm, and was for a time well patronized by those who were in general sympathy with the leaders of the association. George Ripley was the teacher in philosophy and mathematics, George P. Bradford in literature, John S. Dwight in Latin and music, Charles A. Dana in Greek and German, and John S. Brown in theoretical and practical agriculture. A six years' course was arranged in preparation for college, and three years were given to acquiring a knowledge of farming. The pupils were required to work one hour each day,

3

the idea being that this was conducive to sound intellectual training.

It would seem, however, that Curtis gave only a part of his time to study, as is indicated in a letter written to his father in June, 1843, and published in the admirable biography by Mr. Edward Cary. "My life is summery enough here," he writes. "We breakfast at six, and from seven to twelve I am at work. After dinner, these fair days permit no homage but to their beauty, and I am fain to woo their smiles in the shades and sunlights of the woods. A festal life for one before whom the great sea stretches which must be sailed ; yet this summer air teaches life-navigation, and I listen to the flowing streams, and to the cool rush of the winds among the trees, with an increase of that hope which is the only pole-star of life."

At Brook Farm, Curtis studied Greek, German, music, and agriculture. The teaching was of the best, as good as could have been had in any college of the country at that time, and was thorough and efficient. Much more of freedom was allowed the students than was usual elsewhere, both as to conditions of study and recitation, and as to the relations of the pupils to the instructors. The young people in the school were treated as friends and companions by their teachers ; but this familiarity did not breed contempt for the instructors or indifference to the work of the

4

school. On the other hand, it secured an unusual degree of enthusiasm both for the teachers and for the subjects pursued. The work of the school went on with somewhat less of system than is thought desirable in most places of instruction; but in this instance the results justified the methods pursued. The teachers were such as could command success by their personal qualities and by their enthusiastic devotion to their work.

The two years spent at Brook Farm formed an important episode in the life of George William Curtis. It is evident that he did not surrender himself to the associationist idea, even when he was a boarder at Brook Farm and a member of its school. He loved the men and women who were at the head of the community; he found the life attractive and genial, the atmosphere was conducive to his intellectual and spiritual development; but he did not surrender himself to the idea that the world can be reformed in that manner. In a degree he was a curious looker-on; and in a still larger way he was a sympathetic, but not convinced, friend and well-wisher. If not a member, he retained throughout life his interest in this experiment, and remembered with delight the years he spent there. He more than once spoke in enthusiastic terms of Brook Farm, and gave its theories and its practice a sympathetic interpretation. In one of his " Easy Chair " essays of 1869 he described the best side of its life:

" There is always a certain amount of oddity latent in society which rushes to such an enterprise as a natural vent; and in youth itself there is a similar latent and boundless protest against the friction and apparent unreason of the existing order. At the time of the Brook Farm enterprise this was everywhere observable. The freedom of the antislavery reform and its discussions had developed the 'come-outers,' who bore testimony in all times and places against church and state. Mr. Emerson mentions an apostle of the gospel of love and no money who preached zealously but never gathered a large church of believers. Then there were the protestants against the sin of flesh-eating, refining into curious metaphysics upon milk, eggs, and oysters. To purloin milk from the udder was to injure the maternal affections of the cow; to eat eggs was Feejee cannibalism and the destruction of the tender germ of life, to swallow an oyster was to mask murder. A still selecter circle denounced the chains that shackled the tongue and the false delicacy that clothed the body. Profanity, they said, is not the use of forcible and picturesque words; it is the abuse of such to express base passions and emotions. So indecency cannot be affirmed of the model of all grace, the human body. . . .

6

"These were harmless freaks and individual fantasies. But the time was like the time of witchcraft. The air magnified and multiplied every appearance, and exceptions and idiosyncrasies and ludicrous follies were regarded as the rule, and as the logical masquerade of this foul fiend Transcendentalism, which was evidently unappeasable, and was about to devour manners, morals, religion, and common-sense. If Father Lamson or Abby Folsom were borne by main force from an antislavery meeting, and the non-resistants pleaded that these protestants had as good right to speak as anybody, and that what was called their senseless babble was probably inspired wisdom, if people were only heavenly minded enough to understand it, it was but another sign of the impending anarchy. And what was to be said—for you could not call them old dotards—when the younger protestants of the time came walking through the sober streets of Boston and seated themselves in concert-halls and lecture-rooms with hair parted in the middle and falling upon their shoulders, and clad in garments such as no known human being ever wore before—garments which seemed to be a compromise between the blouse of the Paris workman and the *peignoir* of a possible sister? For tailoring underwent the same revision to which the whole philosophy of life was subjected, and one ardent youth, asserting that the human form it-

7

self suggested the proper shape of its garments, caused trowsers to be constructed that closely fitted the leg, and bore his testimony to the truth in coarse crash breeches.

"These were the ludicrous aspects of the intellectual and moral fermentation or agitation that was called Transcendentalism. And these were foolishly accepted by many as its chief and only signs. It was supposed that the folly was complete at Brook Farm, and it was indescribably ludicrous to observe reverend Doctors and other Dons coming out to gaze upon the extraordinary spectacle, and going about as dainty ladies hold their skirts and daintily step from stone to stone in a muddy street, lest they be soiled. The Dons seemed to doubt whether the mere contact had not smirched them. But droll in itself, it was a thousandfold droller when Theodore Parker came through the woods and described it. With his head set low upon his gladiatorial shoulders, and his nasal voice in subtle and exquisite mimicry reproducing what was truly laughable, yet all with infinite *bonhomie* and with a genuine superiority to small malice, he was as humorous as he was learned, and as excellent a mime as he was noble and fervent and humane a preacher. On Sundays a party always went from the Farm to Mr. Parker's little country church. He was there exactly what he was afterwards when he preached to thousands of eager people in the Boston Music-hall; the same plain, simple, rustic, racy man. His congregation were his personal friends. They loved him and admired him and were proud of him; and his geniality and tender sympathy, his ample knowledge of things as well as of books, drew to him all ages and sexes and conditions.

"The society at Brook Farm was composed of every kind of person. There were the ripest scholars, men and women of the most æsthetic culture and accomplishment, young farmers, seamstresses, mechanics, preachers — the industrious, the lazy, the conceited, the sentimental. But they were associated in such a spirit and under such conditions that, with some extravagance, the best of everybody appeared, and there was a kind of high *esprit de corps* — at least, in the earlier or golden age of the colony. There was plenty of steady, essential, hard work, for the founding of an earthly paradise upon a rough New England farm is no pastime. But with the best intention, and much practical knowledge and industry and devotion, there was in the nature of the case an inevitable lack of method, and the economical failure was almost a foregone conclusion. But there was never such witty potato-patches and such sparkling cornfields before or since. The weeds were scratched out of the ground to the music of Tennyson or Browning, and the nooning was an hour as gay and bright as any brilliant midnight at Ambrose's. But in the midst of all was one figure, the practical farmer, an honest neighbor who was not drawn to the enterprise by any spiritual attraction, but was hired at good wages to superintend the work, and who always seemed to be regarding the whole affair with the most good-natured wonder as a prodigious masquerade. . . .

"But beneath all the glancing colors, the lights and shadows of its surface, it was a simple, honest, practical effort for wiser forms of life than those in which we find ourselves. The criticism of science, the sneer of literature, the complaint of experience is that man is a miserably half-developed being, the proof of which is the condition of human society, in which the few enjoy and the many toil. But the enjoyment cloys and disappoints, and the very want of labor poisons the enjoyment. Man is made, body and soul. The health of each requires reasonable exercise. If every man did his share of the muscular work of the world, no other man would be overwhelmed by it. The man who does not work imposes the necessity of harder toil upon him who does. Thereby the first steals from the last the opportunity of mental culture — and at last we reach a world of pariahs and patricians, with all the inconceivable sorrow and suffering that surround us. Bound fast by the brazen age, we can see that the way back to the age of gold lies through justice, which will substitute co-operation for competition.

"That some such generous and noble thought inspired this effort at practical Christianity is most probable. The Brook Farmers did not interpret the words, 'the poor ye have always with ye,' to mean, 'ye must always keep some of you poor.' They found the practical Christian in him who said to his neighbor, 'Friend, come up higher.' But, apart from any precise and defined intention, it was certainly a very alluring prospect —that of life in a pleasant country, taking exercise in useful toil, and surrounded with the most interesting and accomplished people. Compared with other efforts upon which time and money and industry are lavished, measured by Colorado and Nevada speculations, by California gold-washing, by oil-boring, and by the stock exchange, Brook Farm was certainly a very reasonable and practical enterprise, worthy of the hope and aid of generous men and women. The friendships that were formed there were enduring. The devotion to noble endeavor, the sympathy with all that is most useful to men, the kind patience and constant charity that were fostered there, have been no more lost than grain dropped upon the field. It is to the Transcendentalism that seemed to so many good souls both wicked and absurd that some of the best influences of American life to-day are due. The spirit that was concentrated at Brook Farm is diffused, but it is not lost. As an organized effort, after many downward changes, it failed; but those who remember the Hive, the Eyrie, the Cottage; when Margaret Fuller came and talked, radiant with bright humor; when Emerson and Parker and Hedge joined the circle for a night or a day; when those who may not be publicly named brought beauty and wit and social sympathy to the feast; when the practical possibilities of life seemed fairer, and life and character were touched ineffaceably with good influence, cherish a pleasant vision which no fate can harm, and remember with ceaseless gratitude the blithe days of Brook Farm."

Curtis returned to the same subject in 1874, in discussing Frothingham's biography of George Ripley. Some of the errors into which writers about Brook Farm had fallen he undertook to correct, to point out the real character of the association, and its effort at the improvement of society.

" The Easy Chair describes Brook Farm as an Arcadia, for such in effect was the intention, and such is the retrospect to those who recall the hope from which it sprang. . . . The curious visitors who came to see poetry in practice saw with dismay hard work on every side, plain houses and simple fare, and a routine with little æsthetic aspect. Individual whims in dress and conduct, however, were exceptional in the golden age or early days at Brook Farm, and those are wholly in error who suppose it to have been a grotesque colony of idealogues. It was originally a company of highly educated and refined persons, who felt that the immense disparity of condition and opportunity in the world was a practical injustice, full of peril for society, and that the vital and fundamental principle of Christianity was universally rejected by Christendom as impracticable. Every person, they held, is entitled to mental and moral culture, but it is impossible that he should enjoy his rights as long as all the hard physical work of the world is done by a part only of its inhabitants. Were that work limited to what is absolutely necessary, and shared by all, all would find an equal opportunity for higher cultivation and development, and the evil of an unnatural and cruelly artificial system of society would disappear. It was a thought and a hope as old as humanity, and as generous as old. No common mind would have cherished such a purpose, no mean nature have attempted to make the dream real. The practical effort failed in its immediate object, but, in the high purposes it confirmed and strengthened, it had remote and happy effects which are much more than personal.

"It is an error to suppose that many of the more famous 'Transcendentalists' were of the

Brook Farm company. Mr. Emerson, for instance, was never there except as a visitor. Margaret Fuller was often a visitor, and passed many
days together as a guest, but she was never, except in sympathy, one of the Brook Farmers.
Theodore Parker was a neighbor, and had friendly relations with many of the fraternity, but he
seldom came to the farm. Meanwhile the enterprise was considered an unspeakable folly, or
worse, by the conservative circle of Boston. In
Boston, where a very large part of the 'leaders'
of society in every way were Unitarians, Unitarian conservatism was peremptory and austere.
The entire circle of which Mr. Ticknor was the
centre or representative, the world of Everett and
Prescott and their friends, regarded Transcendentalism and Brook Farm, its fruit, with good-
humored wonder as with Prescott, or with severe
reprobation as with Mr. Ticknor. The general
feeling in regard to Mr. Emerson, who was ac-
counted the head of the school, is well expressed
by John Quincy Adams in 1840. The old gentleman, whose glory is that he was a moral and
political gladiator and controversialist, deplores
the doom of the Christian Church to be always
racked with differences and debates, and after
speaking of 'other wanderings of mind' that 'let
the wolf into the fold,' proceeds to say: 'A
young man named Ralph Waldo Emerson, a son
of my once-loved friend William Emerson, and a

classmate of my lamented son George, after failing in the every-day avocations of a Unitarian preacher and school-master, starts a new doctrine of Transcendentalism, declares all the old revelations superannuated and worn out, and announces the approach of new revelations.' Mr. Adams was just on the eve of his antislavery career, but he continues: 'Garrison and the non-resistant Abolitionists, Brownson and the Marat Democrats, phrenology and animal magnetism, all come in, furnished each with some plausible rascality as an ingredient for the bubbling caldron of religion and politics.' C. P. Cranch, the poet and painter, was a relative of Mr. Adams, and then a clergyman; and the astonished ex-President says: 'Pearse Cranch, *ex ephebis*, preached here last week, and gave out quite a stream of Transcendentalism most unexpectedly.'

"This was the general view of Transcendentalism and its teachers and disciples held by the social, political, and religious establishment. The separation and specialty of the 'movement' soon passed. The leaders and followers were absorbed in the great world of America; but that world has been deeply affected and moulded by this seemingly slight and transitory impulse. How much of the wise and universal liberalizing of all views and methods is due to it! How much of the moral training that revealed itself in the war was part of its influence! The transcendental or spiritual philosophy has been strenuously questioned and assailed. But the life and character it fostered are its sufficient vindication."

The school at Brook Farm brought together there a large number of bright young people, and they formed one of the chief characteristics of the place. The result was that the life was one of much amusement and healthy pleasure, as George P. Bradford has said:

"We were floated away by the tide of young life around us. There was always a large number of young people in our company, as scholars, boarders, etc., and this led to a considerable mingling of amusement in our life; and, moreover, some of our company had a special taste and skill in arranging and directing this element. So we had very varied amusements suited to the different seasons — tableaux, charades, dancing, masquerades, and rural fêtes out-of-doors, and in winter, skating, coasting, etc."

In her "Years of Experience," Mrs. Georgiana Bruce Kirby, who was at Brook Farm for very nearly the same period as Curtis, has not only given an interesting account of the social life there, but she has especially described the entertainments mentioned by Mr. Bradford. Two of these occasions, when Curtis was a leading participant, she mentions with something of detail.

"At long intervals in what most would call

our drudgery," she says, "there came a day devoted to amusement.   Once we had a masquerade picnic in the woods, where we were thrown
into convulsions of laughter at the sight of
George W. Curtis dressed as Fanny Ellsler, in a
low-necked, short-sleeved, book-muslin dress and
a tiny ruffled apron, making courtesies and pirou-
etting down the path.   It was much out of character that I, a St. Francis squaw, in striped shirt,
gold beads, and moccasins, should be guilty of such
wild hilarity.   Ora's movements were free and
graceful in white Turkish trousers, a rich Oriental
head-dress, and Charles Dana's best tunic, which
reached just below her knee.   She was the ob-
served of all observers.

"In the midwinter we had a fancy-dress ball
in the parlors of the Pilgrim House, when the
Shaws and Russells, generous friends of the association, came attired as priests and dervishes.
The beautiful Anna Shaw was superb as a port-
ly Turk in quilted robe, turban, mustache, and
cimeter, and bore herself with grave dignity.

"George W. Curtis, as Hamlet, led the quad-
rille with Carrie Shaw as a Greek girl.   His sad
and solemn 'reverence' contrasted charmingly
with her sunny ease.   He acted the Dane to the
life, his bearing, the melancholy light in his eyes,
his black-plumed head-cover, and his rapier glittering under his short black cloak, which fell
apart in the dance, were all perfect.   It was a

B   17

picture long to be remembered, and as long as I could watch these two I had no desire to take part in the dance myself."

Another phase of Curtis's life at Brook Farm she also mentions, and it gives a new insight into his character. The occasion described was a social Sunday evening spent in the parlor of the Eyrie:

" At supper it was whispered that George W. Curtis would sing at the Eyrie, upon which several young men volunteered to assist with the dishes. My services were also cordially accepted. . . . And now we ascended the winding, moonlit path to the Eyrie, where Curtis was already singing. We went up the steps of the building cautiously, lest a note of the melody which floated through the open French windows should be lost to us. Entering the large parlor, we found not only the chairs and sofas occupied, but the floor well covered with seated listeners.

" I did not at first recognize the operatic air, so admirably modified and retarded it was, and its former rapid words replaced by a sad and touching theme, which called for noble endurance in one borne down by suffering. The accompaniment consisted of simple chords and arpeggios, a very plain and sufficient background. Curtis, though not yet twenty—not nineteen, if I remember rightly—had a grave and mature appearance. He was full of poetic sensibility, and

his pure, rich voice had that sympathetic quality
that penetrates to the heart. . . . Curtis was not
ever guilty of singing a comic song. It would
indeed have been most inappropriate to our intensely earnest mood. Often his brother would
join him in a duet with his agreeable tenor.

"Low praises and half-spoken thanks were
murmured as the grave and gracious young
friend, at the expiration of an hour, swung round
on the piano-stool and attempted to make his
exit."

In his "Cheerful Yesterdays," Colonel T. W.
Higginson has described the same life as an on-
looker. Although not a member of the community at Brook Farm, he was somewhat in sympathy with it—at least, with the people of whom
it was composed. At the time he was living in
Brookline and teaching the children of a cousin.
"Into this summer life," he writes, "there occasionally came delegations of youths from Brook
Farm. Among these were George and Burrill
Curtis, and Larned, with Charles Dana—all pre-
sentable and agreeable, but the first three peculiarly costumed. It was then very common for
young men in college and elsewhere to wear what
were called blouses — a kind of hunter's frock,
made at first of brown holland, belted at the waist,
these being gradually developed into garments of
gay-colored chintz, sometimes, it was said, an economical transformation of their sisters' skirts or

petticoats. All the young men of this party but Dana wore these gay garments, and bore on their heads little round and visorless caps with tassels."

"I was but twice at Brook Farm," Higginson continues, "once driving over there to a fancy ball at 'the Community,' as it was usually called, where my cousin Barbara Channing was to appear in a pretty Creole dress made of madras handkerchiefs. She was enthusiastic about Brook Farm, where she went often, being a friend of Mrs. Ripley. . . . Again, I once went for her in summer and stayed for an hour, watching the various interesting figures, including George William Curtis, who was walking about in shirt-sleeves, with his boots over his trousers, yet was escorting a young maiden with that elegant grace which never left him. It was a curious fact that he, who was afterwards so eminent, was then held wholly secondary in interest to his handsome brother Burrill, whose Raphaelesque face won all hearts, and who afterwards disappeared from view in England. But if I did not see much of Brook Farm on the spot, I met its members frequently at the series of exciting meetings for Social Reform in Boston."

Other reminiscences of Brook-Farmers tell of the Curtis brothers and their active part in the amusements of the place. They were leaders among the young people, and they had those gifts of social guidance which placed them at the head of whatever entertainment was being organized. Their grace of manner and beauty of face and figure also won consideration for them, so that they were accepted into every circle and found friends on every hand. It seems that Burrill was at this time regarded as the handsomer, but in time George gained the chief place in this regard. Their courtesy led them to help those whose labors were hard, to aid the women in the laundry at their tasks, and to assist them in hanging out the clothes on washing-days. In the evening the clothes-pins which had been thrust into a pocket found their way to the floor of the dancing-room.

One of the members of the community has written that the brothers "looked like young Greek gods." "Burrill, the elder, with a typical Greek face and long hair falling to his shoulders in irregular curls," she says, "I remember as most unconscious of himself, interested in all about him, talking of the Greek philosophers as if he had just come from one of Socrates' walks, carrying the high philosophy into his daily life, helping the young people with hard arithmetic lessons, trimming the lamps daily at the Eyrie, where the two brothers came to live (my sister saw George assisting him one day, and occasionally, she says, he turned his face with a disgusted expression, trying to puff away the disagreeable odor), never losing control of himself, with the kindest manner to every person. He and George seemed very companionable and fond of each other.

"George, though only eighteen, seemed much older, like a man of twenty-five, possibly, with a peculiar elegance, if I may so express it; great and admirable attention, as I recollect, when listening to any one; courteous recognition of others' convictions and even prejudices; and never a personal animosity of any kind—a certain remoteness of manner, however, that I think prevented persons from becoming acquainted with him as easily as with Burrill."

In his "Memories of Brook Farm," Dr. John T. Codman mentions the occasional returns of Curtis to the Farm after he had left it, and says he heard him singing the "Erl King," "Kathleen Mavourneen," and "Good-night to Julia" "in his inimitable manner." Everything goes to indicate that he was a favorite, not only with the younger persons, but with those who were older. He had already developed a mature thoughtfulness, and gave indications of his power as a writer and speaker. His fondness for music, and his enthusiastic study of it under Dwight's leadership is an indication of that æsthetic appreciation which he kept through life, and which appeared in his mastership of prose style.

At first each one helped himself to the food placed on the table in the dining-room at the Hive, or those at the table helped each other.

In this way more or less confusion was produced, and the results were unsatisfactory. Accordingly, Charles Dana organized a group, including Curtis and other young men of character and good breeding, to act as waiters. Dana took his place at the head of this group of voluntary servants, who performed their duties with grace and alacrity. "It is hardly necessary to observe," says Mrs. Kirby, "that the business was henceforth attended to with such courtly grace and such promptness that the new *régime* was applauded by every one, although it did appear at first as if we were all engaged in acting a play. The group, with their admired chief, took dinner, which had been kept warm for them, afterwards, and were themselves waited upon with the utmost consideration."

II

WHILE at Brook Farm, Curtis was on intimate terms with most of the persons there. He greatly admired Mr. and Mrs. Ripley, and he frequently wrote to Mrs. Ripley and made of her a sort of mother-confessor. He also highly appreciated the scholarly qualities of Charles Dana, and his capacity as a leader. In his letters he frequently mentions "the two Charleses," who were Charles Dana and Charles Newcomb.

The latter has been described by Dr. Codman as "the mysterious and profound, with his long, dark, straight locks of hair, one of which was continually being brushed away from his forehead as it continually fell; with his gold-bowed eye-glass, his large nose and peculiar blue eyes, his spasmodic expressions of nervous horror, and his cachinnatious laugh." Newcomb was for many years a resident of Providence, afterwards finding a home in England and in Paris. He was early a member of Brook Farm—a solitary, self-involved person, preferring to associate with children rather than with older persons. He read much in the literature of the mystics, and was laughingly said to prefer paganism to Christianity. He had a feminine temperament, was full of sensibility, and of an indolent turn of mind. Emerson was attracted to him, and at one time had great expectations concerning his genius. His paper, published in *The Dial*, under the title of "The Two Dolons," was much admired by some of the Trancendentalists when it was printed there; and it is referred to by Hawthorne in his "Hall of Phantasy." In June, 1842, Emerson wrote to Margaret Fuller: "I wish you to know that I have 'Dolon' in black and white, and that I account Charles N. a true genius; his writing fills me with joy, so simple, so subtle, and so strong is it. There are sentences in 'Dolon' worth the printing of *The Dial* that they may go forth." This paper was given him for publication at Emerson's urgent request, and it is not known that Newcomb has published anything else. In 1850 Emerson said he had come to doubt Newcomb's genius, having found that he did not care for an audience.

Another person of whom Curtis speaks is Isaac Hecker, who became a member of the Catholic Church, under the guidance of Orestes Brownson. He was born in New York City, was brought up under Methodist auspices, became a baker, developed a strong taste for philosophy, and went to Brook Farm at the age of twenty-two. He remained for a few months as a student, and then tried Alcott's Fruitlands for a fortnight. He was naturally of an ascetic turn of mind, loved mystic books and philosophy, and found in the Catholic Church his true religious home. He secured at Brook Farm a kind of culture which he much needed, and his abilities were seen by those around him. After his return to New York, Ripley, and Charles Lane, of Fruitlands, wrote him in a way which indicated their faith in him as a man of judgment and liberal aims. He spent some months in Concord, had George P. Bradford for his tutor, and he rented a room of Mrs. Thoreau, the mother of Henry D. Thoreau. There again he met the Curtis brothers; but soon after he went to Holland to prepare for the priesthood, and then entered upon his life-work. A curious phase in the life of this time was the effort of Hecker to convert Curtis to his own way of religious thinking, as Curtis relates in his letters. Even more singular was the attempt of Hecker to persuade Thoreau into the Catholic Church. Mr. Sanborn has read a letter in which he proposed to Thoreau to travel on foot with him in Europe. His real purpose seems to have been to get Thoreau away from Protestants, and among the influences of the Catholic churches and traditions, and thus to make a convert of him. In a letter printed in Father Elliott's biography of Father Hecker, Curtis gave an account of his acquaintance with the founder of the order of the Paulist Fathers.

"WEST NEW BRIGHTON, STATEN ISLAND,
February 28, 1890.

"DEAR SIR,—I fear that my recollections of Father Hecker will be of little service to you, for they are very scant. But the impression of the young man whom I knew at Brook Farm is still vivid. It must have been in the year 1843 that he came to the Farm in West Roxbury, near Boston. He was a youth of twenty-three, of German aspect, and I think his face was somewhat seamed with small-pox. But his sweet and candid expression, his gentle and affectionate manner, were very winning. He had an air of singular refinement and self-reliance combined with a half-eager inquisitiveness, and upon becoming acquainted with him, I told him that he was Ernest the Seeker, which was the title of a story of mental unrest which William Henry Channing was then publishing in *The Dial*.

"Hecker, or, as I always called him and think of him, Isaac, had apparently come to Brook Farm because it was a result of the intellectual agitation of the time which had reached and touched him in New York. He had been bred a baker, he told me, and I remember with what satisfaction he said to me, 'I am sure of my livelihood, because I can make good bread.' His powers in this way were most satisfactorily tested at the Farm, or, as it was generally called, 'the Community,' although it was in no other sense a community than an association of friendly workers in common. He was drawn to Brook Farm by the belief that its life would be at least agreeable to his convictions and tastes, and offer him the society of those who might answer some of his questions, even if they could not satisfy his longings.

"By what influence his mind was first affected by the moral movement known in New England as Transcendentalism, I do not know. Probably he may have heard Mr. Emerson lecture in New York, or he may have read Brownson's 'Charles Elwood,' which dealt with the questions that engaged his mind and conscience. But among the many interesting figures at Brook Farm I recall none more sincerely absorbed than Isaac Hecker in serious questions. The merely æsthetic aspects of its life, its gayety and social pleasures, he regarded good-naturedly, with the air of a spectator who tolerated rather than needed or enjoyed them. There was nothing ascetic or severe in him, but I have often thought since that his feeling was probably what he might have afterwards described as a consciousness that he must be about his Father's business.

"I do not remember him as especially studious. Mr. Ripley had classes in German philosophy and metaphysics, in Kant and Spinoza, and Isaac used to look in, as he turned wherever he thought he might find answers to his questions. He went to hear Theodore Parker preach in the Unitarian Church in the neighboring village of West Roxbury. He went to Boston, about ten miles distant, to talk with Brownson, and to Concord to see Emerson. He entered into the working life at the Farm, but always, as it seemed to me, with the same reserve and attitude of observation. He was the dove floating in the air, not yet finding the spot on which his foot might rest.

"The impression that I gathered from my intercourse with him, which was boyishly intimate and affectionate, was that of all 'the apostles of the newness,' as they were gayly called, whose

28

counsel he sought, Brownson was the most satisfactory to him. I thought then that this was due to the authority of Brownson's masterful tone, the definiteness of his views, the force of his 'understanding,' as the word was then philosophically used in distinction from the reason. Brownson's mental vigor and positiveness were very agreeable to a candid mind which was speculatively adrift and experimenting, and, as it seemed to me, which was more emotional than logical. Brownson, after his life of varied theological and controversial activity, was drawing towards the Catholic Church, and his virile force fascinated the more delicate and sensitive temper of the young man, and, I have always supposed, was the chief influence which at that time affected Hecker's views, although he did not then enter the Catholic Church.

" He was a general favorite at Brook Farm, always equable and playful, wholly simple and frank in manner. He talked readily and easily, but not controversially. His smile was singularly attractive and sympathetic, and the earnestness of which I have spoken gave him an unconscious personal dignity. His temperament was sanguine. The whole air of the youth was that of goodness. I do not think that the impression made by him forecast his career, or, in any degree, the leadership which he afterwards held in his Church. But everybody who knew

him at that time must recall his charming amia-
bility.

"I think that he did not remain at Brook Farm
for a whole year, and when later he went to Bel-
gium to study theology at the seminary of Mons
he wrote me many letters, which, I am sorry to
say, have disappeared. I remember that he la-
bored with friendly zeal to draw me to his
Church, and at his request I read some writing
of St. Alphonse of Liguori. Gradually our correspondence declined when I was in Europe, and
was never resumed; nor do I remember seeing
him again more than once, many years ago.
There was still in the clerical figure, which was
very strange to me, the old sweetness of smile
and address; there was some talk of the idyllic
days, some warm words of hearty good-will, but
our interests were very different, and, parting,
we went our separate ways. For a generation
we lived in the same city, yet we never met.
But I do not lose the bright recollection of
Ernest the Seeker, nor forget the frank, ardent,
generous, manly youth, Isaac Hecker.

"Very truly yours,
"GEORGE WILLIAM CURTIS."

One of the teachers at Brook Farm was George
P. Bradford, who left there at about the same
time Curtis did, and was then a tutor in Concord. When the account of philosophy in Bos-

ton was left uncompleted by Ripley, Bradford
finished it for the "Memorial History of Boston." While living in the Old Manse in Concord, Hawthorne wrote to Margaret Fuller: "I
have thought of receiving a personal friend, and
a man of delicacy, into my household, and have
taken a step towards that object. But in doing
so I was influenced far less by what Mr. Bradford is than by what he is not; or, rather, his
negative qualities seem to take away his personality, and leave his excellent characteristics to be
fully and fearlessly enjoyed. I doubt whether
he be not precisely the rarest man in the world."
Mrs. Hawthorne wrote of Bradford, that "his
beautiful character makes him perennial in interest." After the death of Bradford, Curtis
wrote of him in one of the most appreciative of
the biographical papers which the "Easy Chair"
gave to the public:

"Whoever had the happiness of knowing the
late George P. Bradford, upon reading that he
was the son of a stout sea-captain of Duxbury,
must have recalled Charles Lamb's description of
one of his comrades at the old South Sea House
—'like spring, gentle offspring of blustering winter.' A more gentle, truthful, generous, constant, high-minded, accomplished man, or, as
Emerson, his friend of many years, said of
Charles Sumner, 'a whiter soul,' could not be
known. However wide and various and de-

lightful your acquaintance may have been, if you knew George Bradford, you knew a man unlike all others. His individuality was entirely unobtrusive, but it was absolute.

"The candor of his nature refused the least deceit, and rejected every degree of indirectness without consciousness or effort. His admirable mind, the natural loftiness of his aim, his instinctive sympathy with every noble impulse and humane endeavor, his fine intellectual cultivation, all made him the friend of the best men and women of his time and neighborhood, and none among them but acknowledged the singular charm of a companion who asserted his convictions by his character, and with whom controversy was impossible. Mr. Bradford had the temperament, the tastes, and the acquirements of a scholar; a fondness for nature, and a knowledge which made him her interpreter; yet still more obvious were the social sympathy and tenderness of feeling that brought him into intimate personal relations which time could not touch.

"Something in his appearance and manner, a half-shrinking and smiling diffidence, an unworn and childlike ardor and unconsciousness, a freshness of feeling and frankness of address, invested his personality with what we call quaintness. He was always active, even to apparent restlessness, not from nervous excitement, but from fulness of life and sympathy. You might think of a hum-

ming-bird darting from flower to flower, of a
honey-bee happy in a garden. He graduated at
Harvard, meaning to be a clergyman, but the
publicity, the magisterial posture, the incessant
constraint of the liberty which he valued more
than all else, with the lack of oratorical gifts and
of the self-asserting disposition, soon closed that
career to him; afterwards he was one of the most
cheerful and charming figures at Brook Farm in
its pleasantest day. All his life he was a teacher, mainly of private classes, and generally of
women, now in Plymouth, now in Cambridge,
now elsewhere, but, wherever he was, always beloved and welcomed, and bewailed when he departed.

" Mr. Bradford was unmarried, and there was
a sentiment of solitude in his life, but it was
scarcely more, so affectionate and devoted were
his relations to his kindred and his friends. His
elder sister, Mrs. Samuel B. Ripley, was one of
the most admirably accomplished women in New
England, living for some years in the Old Manse
in Concord in which Hawthorne had lived. Mr.
Ripley was the son of the clergyman who married the widow of his fellow-clergyman who saw
from the Manse the battle at Concord Bridge.
Mr. Bradford was very fond of the old town, and
Mr. Emerson had no friend who was a more welcome or frequent guest than George Bradford,
who came to look after the vegetable garden and

to trim the trees, and in long walks to Walden Pond or Fairhaven Hill to discuss with his host philosophy and poetry and life. The small gains of a teacher were enough for the simple wants of the scholarly gentleman, and after middle life he went often to Europe, and few Americans have ever gone more admirably equipped. He travelled sometimes with a tried comrade, sometimes alone, and a life already full was enriched and enchanted still more by the happy journeys.

" Indeed, the recollection of George Bradford is that of a long life as serene and happy as it was blameless and delightful to others. It was a life of affection and many interests and friendly devotion; but it was not that of a recluse scholar like Edward Fitzgerald, with the pensive consciousness of something desired but undone. George Bradford was in full sympathy with the best spirit of his time. He had all the distinctive American interest in public affairs. His conscience was as sensitive to public wrongs and perilous tendencies as to private and personal conduct. He voted with strong convictions, and wondered sometimes that the course so plain to him was not equally plain to others.

" It was a life of nothing of what we call achievement, and yet a life beneficent to every other life that it touched, like a summer wind laden with a thousand invisible seeds that, dropping everywhere, spring up into flowers and fruit.

BROOK FARM AND CONCORD

It is a name which to most readers of these words is wholly unknown, and which will not be written, like that of so many of the friends of him who bore it, in our literature and upon the memory of his countrymen. But to those who knew him well, and who therefore loved him, it recalls the most essential human worth and purest charm of character, the truest manhood, the most affectionate fidelity. To those who hear of him now, and perhaps never again, these words may suggest that the personal influences which most ennoble and sweeten life may escape fame, but live immortal in the best part of other lives."

Another member of Brook Farm in its earlier period was Minott Pratt, who had been a printer, and the foreman in the office of the *Christian Register*, the Unitarian paper published in Boston. Dr. Codman says of him that he was "a finely formed, large, graceful - featured, modest man. His voice was low, soft, and calm. His presence inspired confidence and respect. Whatever he touched was well done. He was faithful and dignified, and the serenity of his nature welled up in genial smiles. In farm-work he was Mr. Ripley's right hand. They agreed in practical matters, and Ripley deferred to his judgment. His wife was an earnest, strong, faithful worker. They entered into the scheme with fervor." Another Brook Farmer said of him: "No one can ever forget the entire freedom from fret and

fume and worry he evinced, while he never neg-
lected a duty or failed to accomplish his full
share of work. No one can fail to recall how
peaceful and free from criticism his life was, with
what rare fidelity he estimated his fellows, and
how little apparent thought or recognition of
self there was in all his actions. Indeed, the
loveliness of his spirit shone through the bodily
vesture, and his smile itself was a blessing which
one might seek to win, and be proud to have
gained by one's exertions. His presence, in
all the various spheres of active life and industry, had a wonderful educational power upon
both old and young ; and to the influence of
several individuals of similar beauty of character
I attribute the harmony and beauty, in considerable degree, of our Brook Farm life."

Pratt spent the remainder of his life, after the
Brook Farm episode, in Concord, and there he
has, even now, the reputation of having been a
model farmer. He was an extremely modest
man, very little forthputting, gentle in manner,
and most neighborly in spirit. He wrote many
papers for the Concord Farmers' Club, and some
of these were printed in the *Boston Commonwealth*. In that paper, when Mr. Frank B. Sanborn was the editor, he published a series of articles on country life, which were delightful to
read. He was a fine writer, and what he wrote
showed the grace and charm of the man. He

gave much attention to botany, knew all the plants and flowers in Concord, and knew them both as a scientist and poet.

For several years Pratt was in the habit of gathering on the lawn in front of his house, under a large elm-tree, a picnic of such of his Brook Farm associates as he could bring together. Emerson, Phillips, Thoreau, Curtis, George Bradford, and others of note, often attended. The gathering was a delightful one, and it was made an occasion of happy reminiscences and a renewal of old personal ties and affections.

Some of the reminiscences of Brook Farm mention that Curtis walked in the moonlight with Caroline Sturgis, who, over the signature of "Z," contributed a number of poems to *The Dial*. She was an intimate friend of Margaret Fuller, and she afterwards published "Rainbows for Children," "The Magician's Show-box," and other children's books. She married William A. Tappan, who rented to Hawthorne the cottage in which he lived at Lenox. Mrs. Lathrop's book about her mother contains many reminiscences of them. She was a daughter of William Sturgis, a wealthy Boston merchant. A sister, Mrs. Ellen H. Hooper, was also a contributor to *The Dial*, in which appeared her poem beginning with the line:

"I slept and dreamed that life was beauty."

Another well-known poem was written by her:

"She stood outside the gate of heaven and saw them
  entering in."

Colonel Higginson speaks of her as "a woman of
genius," and Margaret Fuller wrote of her from
Rome: "I have seen in Europe no woman more
gifted by nature than she."

Under date of October 25, 1845, Curtis mentions a religious meeting which had been recently held at Brook Farm. This was a reference to
one of the many occasions on which William
Henry Channing conducted religious services
there, for he was listened to with greater satisfaction than any one else who spoke on religious subjects. When the weather was suita-
ble he preached in the grove near the Margaret
Fuller cottage (so called); and on the present
occasion he asked those present to join hands
and to repeat with him a bond of union or confession of faith, and constitute themselves into a
church. Before this time no religious organization had existed at Brook Farm, the utmost liberty of opinion being cultivated there. In fact,
the leaders of the movement had been strongly
opposed to any religious formalism or organized
effort at religious instruction. The freedom of
belief was such that Freethinkers on the one
side, and devout Catholics on the other, were
welcomed with equal cordiality. The majority
of the members were undoubtedly of the "liber-

al " school in theology, and found in the preaching of Theodore Parker the kind of spiritual instruction they desired. At one time there was an enthusiastic interest in the teachings of Swedenborg.

It was the tendency towards what was at once practical and mystical which drew the large majority of the Farmers to the preaching of William Henry Channing, who was one of the most gifted preachers which America has produced. He was imaginative, mystical, and eloquent, liberal in his thinking, progressive in his social ideals, and profoundly religious. He was thoroughly in sympathy with the Associationist movement, and more than any other man he was the spiritual leader and confessor of those who found in that movement a practical realization of their religious convictions.

The organization which began on that Sunday afternoon in October, 1845, continued to exist at Brook Farm until January, 1847, when "The Religious Union of Associationists " was organized in Boston, with Channing as the minister. For a few years it was successful, and it gave union and purpose to the Associationist movement in Boston and the vicinity. A considerable number of the members of Brook Farm were connected with it actively—as officers, members of the choir, or regular attendants.

The organization effected in the pine woods in

so informal a manner was quite in harmony with the Brook Farm spirit and methods. Formalism of every kind was dreaded, but yet there was a deeply religious interest pervading the whole life of the community. At all the meetings held by the Farmers, even at little social gatherings, the conversation was likely to run on high themes. While there was present the utmost freedom of opinion and expression, and while there was the greatest effort to avoid cant and conventional phraseology, yet there was in the community a very strong religious feeling ; and nearly all the members held serious and earnest convictions, to which they were unusually faithful in their daily living.

III

THE relations of Curtis to his teachers at Brook Farm were cordial and appreciative, but they were especially so with John S. Dwight, with whom he studied music. When he left the farm, an intimate and confidential correspondence began between them, and this continued until Curtis went to Europe. After he returned it was resumed, but the interchange of letters was not so frequent. They continued to write to each other almost to the end of Dwight's life, however, and their friendship was always sympathetic and confidential. The letters of Dwight have not been preserved, with two or three exceptions, but those of Curtis still exist in unbroken succession, and are presented to the public in this volume. In these days, when we complain of the decay of letter-writing, they afford a remarkably good specimen of youthful effort in that kind of literature.

To Dwight there were sent by Curtis several poems, which were printed in the *Harbinger*, and he also sent two letters from New York on musical topics. Two of his letters to Dwight from Europe were also printed in the *Harbinger*. After he was settled in New York, Curtis did his part in an effort to get Dwight established in that city. When Dwight began his *Journal of Music*, Curtis wrote for it frequently over the signature of "Hafiz." It is safe to say that these contributions were not paid for, but were the result of a desire to aid his friend in his musical enterprise. They were of the nature of passing comments on the musical performances of the day, but they were worthy of the pages in which they appeared.

John Sullivan Dwight was born in Court Street, Boston, May 13, 1813, the son of Dr. John Dwight and his wife Mary. He was educated at the Derne Street Grammar School and the Boston Latin School, from which he entered Harvard College. As a boy he was a devoted reader of books, studious in his habits, but little inclined to active or practical pursuits. When about fifteen, he began to take an interest in music, and from his father he received the best instruction in that art.

Young Dwight entered Harvard in 1829, and he carried through the studies of the course with a fair degree of success. He gave much attention to music, joined the Pierian Sodality, and was an earnest reader of the best poetry. He gave the class poem on his graduation, in 1832. During his Senior year he taught at Northborough, and following his graduation he spent a year as a tutor in a family at Meadville, Pennsylvania. In the autumn of 1834 he entered the theological school at Harvard, and graduated therefrom in August, 1836, his dissertation being on "The Proper Character of Poetry and Music for Public Worship," which was published in the *Christian Examiner* for that year.

Dwight's interest in music led him to take a leading part in bringing together, in 1837, those recent graduates of the college who were of like mind with himself; and a society was organized for the purpose of promoting its study. In 1840 the name was changed to that of the " Harvard Musical Association "; in 1845 it was incorporated, and in 1848 the place of meeting was transferred to Boston.

It was three years and a half after Dwight left the theological school before he had secured a

pulpit. He preached nearly every Sunday, but
he had become a member of the Transcendental
Club, he was in sympathy with Emerson and
Parker, and the churches did not find his preaching acceptable. He wrote several papers for the
Christian Examiner, and reviewed a number of
books in the same periodical. The first review
of Tennyson published in this country he gave to
the public in that journal. In 1838 he published
in the series of translations edited by George
Ripley, under the general title of "Specimens of
Foreign Standard Literature," a volume of "Select Minor Poems, Translated from the German
of Goethe and Schiller, with Notes." Several of
Dwight's friends aided him in this translation,
especially on the poems of Schiller; but the valuable notes appended were furnished by himself.
The volume was dedicated to Carlyle, who wrote
a characteristic letter in giving his permission,
and a still more interesting one in acknowledg-
ing the receipt of the book.

In May, 1840, Dwight became the minister of
the little Unitarian parish at Northampton, and
the ordination sermon was preached by George
Ripley, the address to the minister being given
by Dr. W. E. Channing. From the first the
people were not fully agreed as to Dwight's
preaching, and the objections gradually increased
as his strong Transcendental habits of thought
began to be more clearly manifest. A few per-

sons of thoughtful and more distinctly spiritual cast of mind were warmly drawn to him, but the majórity grew more and more opposed to him, and he withdrew from the parish after a year and a half. During his stay in Northampton he wrote for *The Dial*, for one or two musical journals, planned several extended literary undertakings, and gave lectures before the American Institute of Instruction and the Harvard Musical Association. In *The Dial* was published one of his sermons, under the title of " Religion of Beauty," and another called " Ideals of Every-day Life." At the end of that on the religion of beauty was printed a poem of Dwight's, which has been often credited to Goethe, and is usually given the title of

"REST

> " Sweet is the pleasure,
>   Itself cannot spoil !
> Is not true leisure
>   One with true toil ?

> "Thou that wouldst taste it,
>   Still do thy best ;
> Use it, not waste it,
>   Else 'tis no rest.

> " Wouldst behold beauty
>   Near thee, all round ?
> Only hath duty
>   Such a sight found.

" Rest is not quitting
  The busy career ;
Rest is the fitting
  Of self to its sphere.

" 'Tis the brook's motion,
  Clear without strife,
Fleeing to ocean
  After its life.

" Deeper devotion
  Nowhere hath knelt;
Fuller emotion
  Heart never felt.

" 'Tis loving and serving
  The Highest and Best!
'Tis onwards! unswerving,
  And that is true rest."

As an intimate friend of George Ripley, Dwight
had discussed with him the project of a community at Brook Farm ; and it was natural that he
should find his place there in November, 1841.
Many years later Dwight said of the purposes of
Ripley, in this effort to improve upon the usual
forms of social life : " His aspiration was to bring
about a truer state of society, one in which human beings should stand in frank relations of
true equality and fraternity, mutually helpful,
respecting each other's occupation, and making
one the helper of the other. The prime idea
was an organization of industry in such a way

that the most refined and educated should show themselves practically on a level with those whose whole education had been hard labor. Therefore, the scholars and the cultivated would take their part also in the manual labor, working on the farm or cultivating nurseries of young trees, or they would even engage in the housework."

In the Brook Farm community, Dwight was one of the leaders, his place being next after Ripley and Dana. In the school he was the instructor in Latin and music. His love for music began to make itself strongly manifest at this time; he brought out all the musical talent which could be developed among the members of the community. Of this phase he said: " The social education was extremely pleasant. For instance, in the matter of music we had extremely limited means or talent, and very little could be done except in a very rudimentary, tentative, and experimental way. We had a singing-class, and we had some who could sing a song gracefully and accompany themselves at the piano. We had some piano music; and, so far as it was possible, care was taken that it should be good—sonatas of Beethoven and Mozart, and music of that order. We sang masses of Haydn and others, and no doubt music of a better quality than prevailed in most society at that date, but that would be counted nothing now. Occasionally we had artists come to visit us. We had delightful readings; and, once in a while, when William Henry Channing was in the neighborhood, he would preach us a sermon."

At this time a musical awakening was taking place in Boston, a genuine taste for and appreciation of Beethoven, Mozart, and Haydn was being developed. Dwight was instrumental in promoting a love for these masters, and out of his classes for their study grew what were called "Mass Clubs." He and his pupils often went into Boston to hear the best music, walking both ways. In *The Dial*, and especially in the *Harbinger*, Dwight wrote with enthusiasm and poetic charm of the merits of classical music. He wrote afterwards that the treatment of music in these periodicals told the time of day far ahead; and "such discussion did at least contribute much to make music more respected, to lift it in the esteem of thoughtful persons to a level with the rest of the humanities of culture, and especially to turn attention to the nobler compositions, and away from that which is but idle, sensual, and vulgar."

To the *Christian Examiner*, *Boston Miscellany*, Lowell's *Pioneer*, and the *Democratic Review*, Dwight was an occasional contributor at this period. His chief literary work, however, was in the form of lectures on musical subjects, especially on the great composers already named. He gave a successful course of musical lectures in New York, and he lectured in a number of other cities.

To the *Harbinger*, which was the organ of Brook Farm after the Fourierite period began, as well as the best advocate of associated life ever published in the country, Dwight was one of the chief contributors. He wrote much in behalf of association, but he also discussed literary topics. His chief contributions were on the subject of music, which was then, as always, so near his heart. He conducted the department devoted to musical criticism and interpretation. During the last year of the publication of the paper at Brook Farm he was associated with Ripley in the editorial management.

In 1847 Brook Farm came to an end. The *Harbinger* was removed to New York, and Ripley was its editor; but it was discontinued in less than two years. Dwight was the Boston correspondent, and continued his editorial connection with the paper. He removed to Boston, continued his interest in association, was an active member of W. H. Channing's "Religious Union of Associationists," was one of the most zealous workers in the organization for promoting associated life, and began to write for the *Daily Chronotype* on musical subjects. In 1849 he edited a department in the *Chronotype* devoted to the interests of association, and he had the assistance of Channing, Brisbane, Dana, and Cranch. This arrangement was continued for only a few months, not proving a success. In 1851 he was for six months the musical editor of the *Boston Commonwealth*, he wrote for *Sartain's Magazine* and other periodicals on musical topics, and he continued to lecture. Ripley and Dana made an earnest effort to secure him a place on one of the daily journals in New York. In February, 1851, Dwight and Mary Bullard, who had been a frequent visitor at Brook Farm, and a member of the choir at Channing's church in Boston, of which Dwight was the musical leader, were married. She was a beautiful and attractive woman, of some musical talent, and of a most unselfish and winning character. They went to live in Charles Street, and there had Dr. O. W. Holmes and his wife for near neighbors.

In April, 1852, Dwight issued the first number of *Dwight's Journal of Music*. He was able to do this with the aid of several of his associationist and musical friends, who generously contributed to a guarantee fund for the purpose. The Harvard Musical Association lent its aid to the project, and made it financially possible. In the first number Dwight said of his purposes and plans:

"Our motive for publishing a musical journal lies in the fact that music has made such rapid progress here within the last fifteen, and even the last ten, years. Boston has been without such a paper, and Boston has thousands of young people who go regularly to hear all the good performances of the best classic models in this art. Its rudiments are taught in all our schools. . . .

"All this requires an organ, a regular bulletin of progress; something to represent the movement, and at the same time help to guide it to the true end. Very confused, crude, heterogeneous is this sudden musical activity in a young, utilitarian people. A thousand specious fashions too successfully dispute the place of true art in the favor of each little public. It needs a faithful, severe, friendly voice to point out steadfastly the models of the true, the ever beautiful, the divine.

"We dare not promise to be all this; but what we promise is, at least, an honest report, week by week, of what we hear and feel and in our poor way understand of this great world of music, together with what we receive through the ears and feeling and understanding of others, whom we trust; with every side-light from the other arts."

What was thus promised was carried out successfully, so far as the spirit and purpose were concerned, for more than thirty years. At first the *Journal of Music* was an eight-page weekly, of about the size of *Harper's Weekly*. After a time it was issued fortnightly, and the number of pages was increased. Though small the *Journal of Music* was varied in contents, and published much that was of great value. The selections from English, French, and German musical publications were well adapted to give music a higher position in American society. Many works of great value were translated for its pages; and whatever new or of importance was taking place or being said in the musical world was faithfully reported. The circulation was small at the best, for the high quality of the paper, and the refusal of the editor to make it an organ of the interests of publishers did not help to bring it widely before the public. Dwight would make no compromises with what was sensational or merely popular.

At the beginning of 1859 the *Journal of Music* was put into the hands of Oliver Ditson & Co., who undertook its publication, paying Dwight a stated salary for his labors upon it. This arrangement relieved him of much drudgery as publisher, which he had hitherto undertaken. The conduct of the paper did not essentially change, but with each number was added a musical composition; the best works of Mendelssohn, Schubert, Wagner, Gluck, Mozart, and many other composers were thus issued. Dwight also did much translating for Ditson, turning into English the words which accompanied some of the best German music.

In July, 1860, Dwight went to Europe for purposes of travel and study. Shortly after his departure his wife was taken ill, and died in a few weeks. The blow nearly crushed him, and it took many months for him to recover himself. In a most sympathetic letter Dr. Holmes told him of the illness, and the scenes which followed:

"I listened to the sweet music which was sung over her as she lay, covered with flowers, in the pleasant parlor of her house, by the voices of those that loved her—I and my wife with me—and then we followed her to Mount Auburn, and saw her laid in the earth, and the blossoms showered down upon her with such tokens of affection and sorrow that the rough men, whose business makes them callous to common impressions, were moved as none of us ever saw them moved before. Our good James Clarke, as you know, conducted the simple service. It was one which none of us who were present will ever forget; and in every heart there was one feeling over all others, that for the far-distant husband, brother, friend, as yet unconscious of the bereavement he was too soon to learn."

Dwight spent a few days in England, was for a fortnight in Paris, went through Switzerland, and then on to Germany. He went to Frankfort, then to Bonn, where he was for some weeks. In Berlin some months were passed, and visits were made to Leipzig, Dresden, Munich, and other cities. He gave much attention to music, taking every opportunity of making himself better acquainted with its traditions and spirit. He then went to Italy, passed on to France, and reached England in July, 1861. Early in September he sailed on the trial trip of the *Great Eastern*, which encountered a fearful storm, and was nearly wrecked. Dwight landed on the Irish coast, made his way back to London, thought of remaining another year in Europe, but finally returned home in November.

In Dwight's absence the *Journal* had been conducted by Henry Ware, a young musical friend. He now established himself in the Studio Building on Tremont Street, and went on with his tasks as usual. He became an active member of the Saturday Club, and was a constant attendant. He helped to organize, in 1863, the Jubilee Concert, at which Emerson read his " Boston Hymn." On the other hand, he severely criticised Gilmore's National Peace Jubilee of 1869.

In 1878 the desire of the Ditson publishing house to make the *Journal of Music* more popular in its character, and more directly helpful to their business interests, led Dwight to transfer its management to the firm of Houghton, Osgood & Co. It was better printed, the list of contributors was enlarged, and in many ways the paper was improved. A number of Dwight's friends promised to stand behind it for a year or two with definite sums of money, that it might be improved, and an effort made to reach a larger public. From some cause, not easy to understand, the response on the part of the public was not large enough to warrant the additional outlay; the list of paid contributors had to be abandoned, and the paper returned gradually to its old ways. In December, 1880, Dwight's friends joined with the musicians of Boston in giving a testimonial concert for the benefit of the paper, which yielded the sum of $6000. In an editorial Dwight said of this expression of interest in his work: "Greetings and warmest signs of recognition, kindliest notes of sympathy (often from most unexpected quarters), prompt, enthusiastic offers of musical service in any concert that might be arranged, poured in upon the editor, who, all at once, found himself the object of unusual attention. Hand and heart were offered wherever he met an old acquaintance; everybody seemed full of the bright idea that had struck somebody just in the nick of time. We never knew we had so many friends."

In September, 1881, the *Journal of Music* came to an end. The position taken by Dwight was not that of the self-seeker; he had no gift for turning his love for the art of music into financial results. He would not lower the critical attitude of his journal for the sake of pleasing the publishers of music; and he would not pretend to a love of those popular forms of music which he held to be inferior in their character. It may be he was not a great critic, certainly he had not the technical knowledge of music which is desirable in its scientific expositor; but his whole soul was in the art, and he gave it the devotion of his life. His preference was for the older composers, and he did not yield a ready homage to those of the newer schools. Of this he speaks in the closing number of his journal: " Startling as the new composers are, and novel, curious, brilliant, beautiful at times, they do not inspire us as we have been inspired before, and do not bring us nearer heaven. We feel no inward call to the proclaiming of the new gospel. We have tried to do justice to these works as they have claimed our notice, and have omitted no intelligence of them which came within the limits of our columns, but we lack motive for entering their doubtful service; we are not ordained their prophet."

Dwight frankly admitted that the causes for the limited success of his journal lay in himself, and said, truly, " We have long realized that we were not made for the competitive, sharp enterprise of modern journalism. The turn of mind which looks at the ideal rather than the practical, and the native indolence of temperament which sometimes goes with it, have made our movements slow. To be the first in the field with an announcement, or a criticism, or an idea, was no part of our ambition; how can one recognize competitors, or enter into competition, and at the same time keep his eye on truth?"

The real value of Dwight's work in his *Journal of Music* was expressed in a letter sent him by Richard Grant White, when the closing number appeared: "I regret very much this close of your valuable editorial labors. You have done great work; and have that consciousness to be sure— some comfort, but it should not be all. There is not a musician of respectability in the country who is not your debtor." In the "Easy Chair" Curtis gave a worthy account of the labors of his friend, and showed how deserving he was of a far greater success than he had reached.

"In the midst of the great musical progress of the country," he wrote, "it is a curious fact that the oldest, ablest, and most independent of musical journals in the United States has just suspended publication, on the eve of the completion of its thirtieth year, for want of adequate support. We mean, of course, *Dwight's Journal of Music*, which ended with an admirably manly, candid, and sagacious, but inevitably pathetic, valedictory from its editor—veteran editor, we should say, if the atmosphere of good music in which he has lived had not been an enchanted air in which youth is perpetually renewed. . . .

A more delightful valedictory it would not be easy to find in the swan song of any journal. . . .

"Mr. Dwight does not say, what the history of music in this country will show, that to no one more than to him are we indebted for the intelligent taste which enjoys the best music. His lectures upon the works of the great Germans at the time of their performance by the Boston Academy of Music in the old Odeon forty years ago were a kind of manual for the intelligent audience. They showed that an elaborate orchestral musical composition might be as serious a work of art, as full of thought and passion, and, in a word, of genius, as a great poem, and that no form of art was more spiritually elevating. They lifted the performance of such music from the category of mere amusement, and asserted for the authors a dignity like that of the master poets. If to some hearers the exposition seemed sometimes fanciful and remote, it was only as all criticism of works of the imagination often seems so. If the spectator sometimes sees in a picture more than the painter consciously intended, it is because the higher power may work with unconscious hands, and because beauty cannot be hidden from the eye made to see it. Beethoven, for instance, had never a truer lover or a subtler interpreter than Dwight, and Dwight taught the teachers, and largely shaped the intelligent appreciation of the unapproached master.

"Those were memorable evenings at the old
Odeon. Francis Beaumont did not more pleasantly recall the things that he and Ben Jonson
had seen done at the Mermaid than an old Brook
Farmer remembers the long walks, eight good
miles in and eight miles out, to see the tall, wil-
lowy Schmidt swaying with his violin at the head
of the orchestra, to hear the airy ripple of Auber's
'Zanetta,' the swift passionate storm of Beethoven's 'Egmont,' the symphonic murmur of woods
and waters and summer fields in the limpid 'Pas-
torale,' or the solemn grandeur of sustained pathetic human feeling in the 'Fifth Symphony.'
The musical revival was all part of the new birth
of the Transcendental epoch, although none
would have more promptly disclaimed any taint
of Transcendentalism than the excellent officers
of the Boston Academy of Music. The building
itself, the Odeon, was the old Federal Street Theatre, and had its interesting associations. . . .
To all there was now added, in the memory of
the happy hearers, the association of the symphony concerts.

"As the last sounds died away, the group of
Brook Farmers, who had ventured from the Arcadia of co-operation into the Gehenna of competition, gathered up their unsoiled garments and
departed. Out of the city, along the bare Tremont road, through green Roxbury and bowery
Jamaica Plain, into the deeper and lonelier coun-

try, they trudged on, chatting and laughing and singing, sharing the enthusiasm of Dwight, and unconsciously taught by him that the evening had been greater than they knew. Brook Farm has long since vanished. The bare Tremont road is bare no longer. Green Roxbury and Jamaica Plain are almost city rather than suburbs. From the symphony concerts dates much of the musical taste and cultivation of Boston. The old Odeon is replaced by the stately Music Hall. The *Journal of Music*, which sprang from the impulse of those days, now, after a generation, is suspended; nor need we speculate why musical Boston, which demands the Passion music of Bach, permits a journal of such character to expire. Amid all these changes and disappearances two things have steadily increased — the higher musical taste of the country, and the good name of the critic whose work has most contributed to direct and elevate it. If, as he says, it is sad that the little bark which the sympathetic encouragement of a few has kept afloat so long goes down before reaching the end of its thirtieth annual voyage, it does not take down with it the name and fame of its editor, which have secured their place in the history of music in America."

From the beginning Dwight was intimately connected with the Harvard Musical Association, which has done so much to promote the interests of music in Boston. He was its first vice-president and chairman of its board of directors. He was active in providing its meetings with attractive musical programmes; about 1844 he secured for it a series of chamber concerts; he took part in procuring the building of Music Hall, and in bringing to it the great organ which was for many years an attraction. From 1855 to 1873 he continuously filled the position of vice-president of the association; and in the latter year was elected president, which place he held until his death. Beginning about 1850 he worked steadily for securing a good musical library, that should be as nearly complete as possible; and his desire was to make this a special feature in the activities of the association. In 1867 a room was secured for it; and in 1869 a suite of rooms was rented for the gatherings, both social and musical, of the members of the association. On his election as president, Dwight went to live in those rooms, cared for the library, and received the members and guests of the association whenever they chose to frequent them. This was in Pemberton Square; but in 1886 there was a removal to Park Square, and another in 1892 to West Cedar Street. Dwight's connection of forty or fifty years with the Harvard Musical Association was most intimate, so that he and the association came to be almost identical in the minds of Boston people. Whatever it accomplished

was through his initiative or with his active co-
operation.

In 1865 Dwight proposed the organization of a
Philharmonic Society among the members of the
association, and also that a series of concerts be
undertaken. This suggestion was carried out,
and the concerts were for many years very successful. In time their place was taken by the
concerts of Theodore Thomas, and the Symphony Concerts generously sustained by Mr. H.
L. Higginson ; but it must be recognized that
Dwight and the Harvard Musical Association
taught the Boston public to appreciate only
those concerts at which the best music was produced.

One special object in the organization of the
Harvard Musical Association was the securing of
a place for music in the curriculum of Harvard
College. That was an object very dear to the
heart of Dwight, and one which he brought forward frequently in the pages of his *Journal of
Music*. He maintained that music was not merely for amusement, but that it is the most human
and spiritual of all the arts, and must find its
place in any systematic effort to secure a full-
rounded culture. In a few years Harvard appointed an instructor in music. Mr. John K.
Paine was called to that position in 1862, and
was made a professor in 1876.

Dwight gave a most generous welcome to all

young musicians of promise as they came forward. Such men as John C. D. Parker, John K.
Paine, Benjamin J. Lang, George W. Chadwick,
Arthur Foote, and William F. Apthorp were generously aided by him ; and the *Journal of Music*
never failed to speak an appreciative word for
them. However Dwight might differ from some
of them, he could recognize their true merits,
and did not fail to make them known to the
public. When Mr. Paine, who had been watched by Dwight with appreciation and approval
from the beginning of his musical career, was
made a professor of music in Harvard University, when his important musical compositions
were published, and when his works were given
fit interpretation in Cambridge and elsewhere,
these events were welcomed by him as true indications of the development of music in this
country.

For many years John S. Dwight was the musical autocrat of Boston, and what he approved
was accepted as the best which could be ob-
tained. His knowledge of music was literary
rather than technical, appreciative rather than
scientific ; but his qualifications were such as to
make him an admirable interpreter of music to
the cultivated public of Boston. What a musical
composition ought to mean to an intelligent person he could make known in language of a fine
literary texture, and with a rare spiritual insight

he voiced its poetic and æsthetic values. If the better-trained musicians of more recent years look upon his musical judgments with somewhat of disapproval, as not being sufficiently technical, they ought not to forget that he prepared the way for them as no one else could have done it, and that he had a fine skill in bringing educated persons to a just appreciation of what music is as an art. As Mr. William F. Apthorp has well said, " his musical instincts and perceptions were, in a certain high respect, of the finest. He was irresistibly drawn towards what is pure, noble, and beautiful, and felt these things with infinite keenness."

Dwight's last years were spent in furthering the interests of the Harvard Musical Association, in writing about his beloved art, and in the society of his many generous friends. He had a talent for friendship, and during his lifetime he was intimately associated with almost every man and woman of note in Boston. He was of a quiet, gentlemanly habit of life, took the world in the way of one who appreciates it and desires to secure from it the most of good, was warmly attached to the children of his friends and found the keenest delight in their presence, loved all that is graceful and beautiful, and devoted himself with unceasing ardor to the art for which he did so much to secure a just appreciation.

On the occasion of his eightieth birthday his

friends and admirers were brought together in the rooms of the Harvard Musical Association. It was a red-letter day in his life, and he greatly appreciated it. A few months later, September 5, 1893, his life came to an end—a life that had been in no way great, but that had been spent in the loving and faithful service of his fellow-men. At his funeral, Mrs. Julia Ward Howe, an intimate friend of many years, read this just and appreciative tribute:

"O Presence reverend and rare,
    Art thou from earth withdrawn?
Thou passest as the sunshine flits
    To light another dawn.

"Surely among the symphonies
    That praise the Ever-blest,
Some strophe of surpassing peace
    Inviteth thee to rest.

"Thine was the treasure of a life
    Heart ripened from within,
Whose many lustres perfected
    What youth did well begin.

"The noble champions of thy day
    Were thy companions meet,
In the great harvest of our race,
    Bound with its priceless wheat.

"Thy voice its silver cadence leaves
    In truth's resistless court,
Whereof thy faithful services
    Her heralds make report.

"Here thou, a watchful sentinel,
    Didst guard the gates of song,
That no unworthy note should pass
    To do her temple wrong.

"Dear are the traces of thy days
    Mixed in these walks of ours;
Thy footsteps in our household ways
    Are garlanded with flowers.

"If we surrender, earth to earth,
    The frame that's born to die,
Spirit with spirit doth ascend
    To live immortally."

The letters contained in this volume give fullest indication of the cordial and intimate relations which existed between Dwight and Curtis. This may be seen more distinctly, perhaps, with the help of a few letters not there given, including two or three written by Dwight to his friend. In a letter to Christopher P. Cranch, the preacher, poet, and artist, written at the time when he was starting his *Journal of Music* on its way, Dwight said: "If you see the Howadji, can you not enlist his active sympathy a little in my cause? A letter now and then from him on music or on art would be a feather in the cap of my enterprise. It is my last, desperate (not very confident), grand *coup d'état* to try to get a living; and I call on all good powers to help me launch the ship, or, rather, little boat."

Curtis seconded his friend's efforts cordially,

subscribed for the new journal, persuaded a number of his friends to subscribe, and wrote frequently for it.   He wrote Dwight this letter of appreciation and advice :

"Your most welcome letter has been received, and its contents have been submitted to the astute deliberations of the editorial conclave [*Tribune*].   We are delighted at the prospect—but we do not love the name.   1st. *Journal of Music* is too indefinite and commonplace.   It will not be sufficiently distinguished from the *Musical Times* and the *Musical World*, being of the same general character.   2d. 'Side-glances' is suspicious.   It 'smells' Transcendentalism, as the French say, and, of all things, any aspect of a clique is to be avoided.

"That is the negative result of our deliberations; the positive is, that you should identify your name with the paper, and call it *Dwight's Musical Journal*, and you might add, *sotto voce*, 'a paper of Art and Literature.'

"Prepend : I shall be very glad to send you a sketch of our winter doings in music, especially as I love Steffanone, although she says, 'I smoke, I chew, I snoof, I drink, I am altogether vicious.' You shall have it Sunday morning.   Give my kindest regards to your wife.   I wish she could sing in your paper."

In a letter written in March, 1882, Dwight expressed to Curtis his appreciation of the most friendly words which the " Easy Chair " had said of him and his work as an editor, in making mention of the fact that the *Journal of Music* had come to the end of its career:

" MY DEAR GEORGE,—With this I send you formal invitation, on the part of the committee of arrangements, for the celebration of the anniversary of the foundation, by Dr. Howe, of the Institution for the Blind. . . . We wish to have an address—not long, say half an hour—partly historical; and we all (committee, director, teachers, pupils) have set our hearts upon having *you* perform that service. It would delight us all; and I know that you would find the occasion, the very sight of those sightless children made so happy, most inspiring. . . . A more responsive audience than the blind themselves cannot be found. Dear George, do think seriously of it, and tell me you will come. Your own wishes in respect to the arrangements and conditions shall in all respects be consulted. But come, if you wish to have a good time, a memorable time, and make a good time for us.

" George, how many times have I been on the point of writing to you since that delightful week we spent at dear old Tweedy's. To me it was a sweet renewal of good old days, and I came away feeling that it must have added some time to my life.   Then, too, I wished to thank you for your most friendly, hearty, and delightful talk about me and my *Journal* in the 'Easy Chair.'   It was so like you, like the dear old George.   I tell you, it made me feel good, as if life wasn't all a fail-ure.   And now I am finding laziness agreeing with me too—too well. . . . And if I were not so very, very *old*, if it were not my fate to have been sent into the world so long before my time, I verily believe I should confess myself over head and ears in love!   At any rate, I love *life*. Yet nearly all my old friends seem to be dead or dying.   When I write you again, I hope to be able to say that I am well at work again; but how?—on what?   Thank God, I am not a 'critic!'"

IV

THE winter of 1843–44 was spent by the Curtis brothers at their father's house in New York. George studied somewhat, heard much music, and read extensively.   In the spring of 1844 they went to live in Concord for purposes of study and recreation.   They wished to know country life, and they regarded it as a desirable part of education that they should become acquainted with practical affairs, and especially with agri-culture.   That tendency of the time which estab-lished Brook Farm and sent Thoreau into the

Concord woods, worked itself out in this desire of two young men to find life at first hand. Colonel Higginson has said of the fresh life started by the transcendental movement: "Under these combined motives I find that I carefully made out, at one time, a project of going into the cultivation of peaches, thus securing freedom for study and thought by moderate labor of the hands. This was in 1843, two years before Thoreau tried a similar project with beans at Walden Pond; and also before the time when George and Burrill Curtis undertook to be farmers at Concord. A like course was actually adopted and successfully pursued through life by another Harvard man a few years older than myself, the late Marston Watson, of Plymouth, Massachusetts. Such things were in the air, and even those who were not swerved by 'the Newness' from their intended pursuits were often greatly as to the way in which they were undertaken."

A letter written by Burrill Curtis, and printed in part by Mr. Cary, gives the reasons for this experiment. He says it was "for the better furtherance of our main and original end — the desire to unite in our own persons the freedom of a country life with moderate out-door occupation, and with intellectual cultivation and pursuits. At Concord we first took up our residence in the family of an elderly farmer, recommended by

69

Mr. Emerson. We gave up half the day (except in hay-time, when we gave the whole day) to sharing the farm - work indiscriminately with the farm-laborers. The rest of the day we devoted to other pursuits, or to social intercourse or correspondence ; and we had a flat-bottomed rowing-boat built for us, in which we spent very many afternoons on the pretty little river. For our second season we removed to another farm and farmer's house, near Mr. Emerson and Walden Pond, where we occupied only a single room, making our own beds, and living in the very simplest and most primitive style. A small piece of ground, which we hired of the farmer, we cultivated for ourselves, raising vegetables only, and selling the superfluous product, and distributing our time much as before."

It was to the house of Captain Nathan Barrett, one mile north of Concord village, west of the river, and overlooking it and its meadows, that the Curtis brothers went. Barrett was born in October, 1797, and was of the seventh generation of his family in the town. His house on Punkatassett Hill was pleasantly located, and the farm was large and well cultivated. Judge John S. Keyes, in the sketch of Barrett's life printed in the second series of the " Memoirs of Members of the Social Circle in Concord," says of him: " His house was the resort of many of the connections of himself and wife, who had there gay

and jolly frolics. He was a captain of the Light
Infantry company of the town. He was naturally of an easy, somewhat indolent disposition,
so that he did little of the harder work of the
farm, but he looked after everything, and he became a thoroughly skilled, practical farmer. His
position as the principal man of his section of
the town, and his own good sense, made him the
leading person in his neighborhood. In person
he was tall, nearly six feet, of large frame, and
good proportions, weighing two hundred pounds,
had a frank, open face, a high forehead, and a
large head. He lived plainly but comfortably;
drove a poor horse but a good carriage to church
and visiting; dressed like his brother farmers
about his work, but neatly and in good style
when at leisure. He loved good fruit, raised it
in large amounts. Neither witty nor humorous,
he was slow to appreciate a joke, but he had a
hearty laugh when he did comprehend it. He
was liberal in his habits, genial in his temperament, and kindly in his disposition. He was
very modest, though firm and reliable; honest in
every fibre, without guile and cunning; thoroughly simple, and yet clear-headed, cool, and
sensible. He was slow in his mental processes,
but no one doubted that he believed all that he
thought and said and did. His apples were not
deaconed, his seeds were sure and reliable, and
his milk was never watered. He never made a

mistake in his accounts but once, and then it was against himself. Everybody knew him and liked him and praised him, and was sorry when he died."

Captain Barrett had a farm of five hundred acres, the largest in the town. He was a large raiser of sheep and milk. He was a deacon in the First Parish Church, thoroughly honest, most neighborly and accommodating in his ways, a loyal citizen, and a true-hearted man. He died in February, 1868, and was lamented by every resident of the town. A typical farmer was Captain Barrett, thoroughly human, loving life and all there is good in it, hard-headed, practical, of sturdy common-sense, faithful to every obligation as he understands it, of a kindly nature, enjoying the doing of good in a plain, simple way, caring little for the supernatural, and yet having a very sturdy faith in the few convictions of a rational religion, without high spiritual insight, he lived his religion in a very honest fashion.

It was quite in keeping with the character of Captain Barrett that he put the Curtis brothers at the task of getting out manure, as almost the first labor he required of them after their arrival on his farm. His idea was to " test their metal," to find what stuff they were made of, and to what extent they were in earnest in their expressed wish to become acquainted with practical agriculture. He spoke of it with glee to his neighbors, that he had put such refined gentlemen at that kind of work. It is needless to say that they bore the test well. They were not domiciled in the farm-house, but in a small cottage somewhat lower down the hill, yet in the immediate neighborhood.

The love of music which George Curtis had developed at Brook Farm continued during his stay in Concord. He sang on occasion, and he often played a flute. The young singer he mentions was Belinda Randall, a sister of John Randall, who published a volume of poems. She was a daughter of Dr. Randall, of Winter Street, Boston, who had a summer place in Stowe. From there she often visited in Concord, perhaps attended school there, and was an intimate friend of Elizabeth Hoar, the betrothed of Edward Emerson, and the sister of Judge Hoar and Senator Hoar, who, when she visited Mrs. Hawthorne, was described as coming "with spirit voice and tread." Belinda Randall has recently died, and left half a million dollars to Harvard University, the Massachusetts Institute of Technology, and the Cambridge Prospect Union. Her sister Elizabeth married Colonel Alfred Cumming, of Georgia, afterwards Governor of Utah. Dr. Randall did not approve of the marriage, and would not have the wedding take place in his house. They were married at the house of Judge Hoar, the father of Elizabeth. She was an excellent musician, but Belinda was the musical genius of the family.

Another person mentioned by Curtis was Almira Barlow, who was at Brook Farm during the time he was there. She had been a Miss Penniman of Brookline, and had the reputation of being a famous beauty. She married David Hatch Barlow, a graduate of Harvard in 1824, and of the Theological School in 1829. Their marriage took place in Brookline about 1830, and they were regarded as the handsomest couple that had been seen in the town. He had a parish in Lynn, and was afterwards settled in Brooklyn; but his habits became irregular, he remained but a short time in any place, and he separated from his wife in 1838. There was much gossip about her, owing to her beauty and her fondness for the society of men.

With Mrs. Barlow at Brook Farm and Concord was her son Francis Channing, born in 1834, who graduated at Harvard in 1855, was a lawyer in New York, rose to the rank of Major-General during the Rebellion, and was afterwards prominent in his profession. He married as his second wife Miss Ellen Shaw, the sister of Colonel Robert G. Shaw and of Mrs. George William Curtis.

Curtis mentions hearing Emerson's address on the anniversary of emancipation in the West Indies, which was delivered in Concord, August

1, 1844. There had existed in Concord for a number of years a Woman's Antislavery Society, of which Mrs. Emerson was a member. Of this society, Mrs. Mary Merrick Brooks was the president, and its most active worker. She invited Emerson to speak on this occasion. He felt that he was excused from political action by virtue of his having been a clergyman, and because of his life as a man of letters. Mrs. Brooks thought otherwise, and she gave him good and urgent reasons why he ought to speak, and to speak then. At last she prevailed, partly because she gave him no rest until he had complied with her request, and partly because his conscience went with her arguments. His attitude hitherto had been such as in part justified the statement made by Carlyle to Theodore Parker in 1843, that the negroes were fit only for slavery, and that Emerson agreed with him.

V

THE second abiding place of Curtis and his brother in Concord was the farm of Edmund Hosmer, which was one-half mile east of Emerson's house, about that distance from Walden Pond, and nearly the same from Hawthorne's Wayside of later years, which faced it, and from which it could be seen. Hosmer was a native of Concord, gave his earlier years to his trade as a tanner, and then spent the remainder of his life as a Concord farmer. He was Emerson's authority on agriculture and gardening more than any one; though in later years Samuel Staples (usually known and spoken of as "Sam") superseded him because he was a nearer neighbor. In 1843, when Emerson wrote to George Ripley declining to join the Brook Farm community, he referred to the opinions of Edmund Hosmer, "a very intelligent farmer and a very upright man in my neighborhood." He gave in full his neighbor's reasons for want of faith in the community idea, that co-operation in farming was not successful, that the word of gentlemen-farmers could not be trusted, that the equal payment of ten cents an hour to every laborer was unjust, and that good work could not be secured if the worker was not directly benefited.

In his notes on the agriculture of Massachusetts, published in *The Dial*, Emerson described his neighbor in these words: "In an afternoon in April, after a long walk, I traversed an orchard where boys were grafting apple-trees, and found the farmer in his cornfield. He was holding the plough, and his son driving the oxen. This man always impresses me with respect, he is so manly, so sweet-tempered, so faithful, so disdainful of all appearances—excellent and reverable in his old weather-worn cap and blue frock bedaubed with

the soil of the field; so honest, withal, that he
always needs to be watched lest he should cheat
himself. I still remember with some shame that
in some dealing we had together a long time ago,
I found that he had been looking to my interest,
and nobody had looked to his part. As I drew
near this brave laborer in the midst of his own
acres, I could not help feeling for him the highest respect. Here is the Cæsar, the Alexander
of the soil, conquering and to conquer, after how
many and many a hard-fought summer's day and
winter's day; not like Napoleon, hero of·sixty
battles only, but of six thousand, and out of every one he has come victor; and here he stands,
with Atlantic strength and cheer, invincible still.
These slight and useless city limbs of ours will
come to shame before this strong soldier, for his
having done his own work and ours too. What
good this man has or has had, he has earned. No
rich father or father-in-law left him any inheri-
tance of land or money. He borrowed the money
with which he bought his farm, and has bred up
a large family, given them a good education, and
improved his land in every way year by year, and
this without prejudice to himself the landlord,
for here he is, a man every inch of him, and reminds us of the hero of the Robin Hood ballad:

> "'Much, the miller's son,
> There was no inch of his body
> But it was worth a groom.'

"Innocence and justice have written their names on his brow. Toil has not broken his spirit. His laugh rings with the sweetness and hilarity of a child; yet he is a man of a strongly intellectual taste, of much reading, and of an erect good sense and independent spirit which can neither brook usurpation nor falsehood in any shape. I walked up and down the field as he ploughed his furrow, and we talked as we walked. Our conversation naturally turned on the season and its new labors." The conversation went on, leading to a discussion of the agricultural survey of the State; Hosmer's opinions of it are quoted as of much worth, and as sounder than anything which the writer could himself say on the subject.

Mr. Sanborn is of the opinion that Edmund Hosmer was described as Hassan in Emerson's fragments on the "Poet and the Poetic Gift," in the complete edition of his poems:

> "Said Saadi, 'When I stood before
> Hassan the camel-driver's door,
> I scorned the fame of Timour brave;
> Timour, to Hassan, was a slave.
> In every glance of Hassan's eye
> I read great years of victory,
> And I, who cower mean and small
> In the frequent interval
> When wisdom not with me resides,
> Worship Toil's wisdom that abides.
> I shunned his eyes, that faithful man's,
> I shunned the toiling Hassan's glance.'"

BROOK FARM AND CONCORD

Hosmer was also described by William Ellery Channing in his " New England " :

" This man takes pleasure o'er the crackling fire,
 His glittering axe subdued the monarch oak ;
 He earned the cheerful blaze by something higher
 Than pensioned blows—he owned the tree he stroke,
 And knows the value of the distant smoke,
 When he returns at night, his labor done,
 Matched is his action with the long day's sun."

Channing spoke of him again as the

" Spicy farming sage,
Twisted with heat and cold and cramped with age,
Who grunts at all the sunlight through the year,
And springs from bed each morning with a cheer.
Of all his neighbors he can something tell,
'Tis bad, whate'er, we know, and like it well !
The bluebird's song he hears the first in spring—
Shoots the last goose bound south on freezing wing."

Hosmer was also one of the farmer friends of Thoreau, who much enjoyed his society and the vigor of his conversation. He is described in the fourteenth chapter of " Walden " as among Thoreau's winter visitors at his hut : " On a Sunday afternoon, if I chanced to be at home, I heard the cronching of the snow made by the step of a long-headed farmer, who from far through the woods sought my house, to have a social ' crack '; one of the few of his vocation who are 'men on their farms'; who donned a frock instead of a

79

professor's gown, and is as ready to extract the moral out of church or state as to haul a load of manure from his barn-yard. We talked of rude and simple things, when men sat about large fires in cold, bracing weather, with clear heads; and when other dessert failed, we tried our teeth on many a nut which wise squirrels have long since abandoned, for those which have the thickest shells are commonly empty." In W. E. Channing's book about Thoreau as the "Poet-Naturalist," there is a passage from his journal in which Thoreau speaks of Hosmer as the last of the farmers worthy of mention. "Human life may be transitory and full of trouble," he says, "but the perennial mind whose survey extends from that spring to this — from Columella to Hosmer — is superior to change. I will identify myself with that which will not die with Columella and will not die with Hosmer."

At Hosmer's house the two young men lived in a single room, and did their own cooking and house-keeping. Mrs. Hosmer furnished them with milk, and they ate crackers, cheese, and fruit largely. They were Grahamites, and used no meat. They read much, and had with them a large number of books. It was their custom here, as well as at Captain Barrett's, to spend much time in the woods. They were enthusiastic students of botany, and came home from their excursions in the woods with their arms loaded with flowers, and often searched out the rarest which could be found in the Walden and Lincoln woods.

It was while the Curtises were living at Hosmer's that they assisted Thoreau in building his hut at Walden Pond. Thoreau says that in March, 1845, he borrowed an axe and went into the woods to build him a house. The axe was procured of Emerson, and he says he returned it sharper than when he received it. He was assisted in building the house, he says, by some of his acquaintances, "rather to improve so good an occasion for neighborliness than from any necessity." These acquaintances were Emerson, Alcott, W. E. Channing, Burrill and George Curtis, Edmund Hosmer and his sons John, Edmund, and Andrew. Thoreau said that he wished the help of the young men because they had more strength than the older ones, and that no man was ever more honored in the character of his raisers than he. It was Thoreau's custom while at Walden to dine on Sundays with Emerson, and to stop at Hosmer's on his way back to the pond, often remaining to supper. After the failure of his experiment at Fruitlands, it was into Hosmer's house that Alcott found himself welcomed; and he was given much of help and encouragement by the farmer and his wife.

VI

AT this time several of the Brook Farmers were living in Concord, and among them were Bradford, Pratt, and Mrs. Barlow; and later on Marianne Ripley, the sister of George Ripley, found a home there, and kept a school for small children. On the third return of the Curtises to Concord, in the summer of 1846, they found a home in the house of Minott Pratt, who was living at the foot of Punkatassett Hill, on the top of which was the house of Captain Barrett. In the same neighborhood lived William Ellery Channing, the poet, whose wife was a sister of Margaret Fuller. They are frequently mentioned in Hawthorne's and his wife's letters from the Old Manse. Pratt's cottage was in a quiet, delightful location; and in the family George Curtis found himself quite at home.

Curtis made a very pleasant impression in Concord, for he was social in his ways, paid much deference to others, and always exemplified a fine etiquette. The brothers are remembered by one person who then knew them as having no mannerisms, and as being perfect gentlemen. His article on Emerson, in the "Homes of American Authors," gave much offence in the town, and by Mrs. Alcott, as well as others, was warmly resented. He was exact enough as to

facts, but he drew from them wrong inferences.
He afterwards said that there was nothing romantic in his paper, and that every incident
mentioned was an actual occurrence. He had
letters from Emerson and Hawthorne before he
wrote his papers on those two authors, to enable
him to verify certain details.

The relations of Curtis and Hawthorne were
cordial if not intimate. In a letter to Hawthorne, written from Europe, Curtis said: " Does
Mrs. Hawthorne yet remember that she sent me
a golden key to the studio of Crawford, in Rome?
I shall never forget that, nor any smallest token
of her frequent courtesy in the Concord days."
In another letter to Hawthorne he speaks of
Concord as " our old home, which is very placid
and beautiful in my memory." In his paper on
Hawthorne, in the " Homes of American Authors," Curtis gave an interesting account of his
acquaintance with that reticent genius during
these Concord days:

" There glimmer in my memory a few hazy
days, of a tranquil and half-pensive character,
which I am conscious were passed in and around
the house, and their pensiveness I know to be
only that touch of twilight which inhered in the
house and all its associations. Beside the few
chance visitors there were city friends occasionally, figures quite unknown to the village, who
came preceded by the steam shriek of the loco-

motive, were dropped at the gate-posts, and were seen no more. The owner was as much a vague name to me as any one.

" During Hawthorne's first year's residence in Concord, I had driven up with some friends to an æsthetic tea at Mr. Emerson's. It was in the winter, and a great wood fire blazed upon the hospitable hearth. There were various men and women of note assembled, and I, who listened attentively to all the fine things that were said, was for some time scarcely aware of a man who sat upon the edge of the circle, a little with-drawn, his head slightly thrown forward upon his breast, and his bright eyes clearly burning under his black brow. As I drifted down the stream of talk, this person, who sat silent as a shadow, looked to me as Webster might have looked had he been a poet — a kind of poetic Webster. He rose and walked to the window, and stood quietly there for a long time, watch-ing the dead, white landscape. No appeal was made to him, nobody looked after him, the con-versation flowed steadily on, as if every one understood that his silence was to be respected. It was the same at table. In vain the silent man imbibed æsthetic tea. Whatever fancies it inspired did not flower at his lips. But there was a light in his eye which assured me that nothing was lost. So supreme was his silence that it presently engrossed me to the exclusion

of everything else.   There was very brilliant discourse, but this silence was much more poetic
and fascinating.   Fine things were said by the
philosophers, but much finer things were implied
by the dumbness of this gentleman with heavy
brows and black hair.   When he presently rose
and went, Emerson, with the 'slow, wise smile' that
breaks over his face like day over the sky, said,
'Hawthorne rides well his horse of the night.'

"Thus he remained in my memory, a shadow,
a phantom, until more than a year afterwards.
Then I came to live in Concord.   Every day I
passed his house, but when the villagers, thinking that perhaps I had some clew to the mystery, said, 'Do you know this Mr. Hawthorne?'
I said, 'No,' and trusted to time.

"Time justified my confidence, and one day I
too went down the avenue and disappeared in
the house.   I mounted those mysterious stairs
to that apocryphal study.   I saw 'the cheerful
coat of paint, and golden-tinted paper-hangings,
lighting up the small apartment; while the shadow of a willow-tree, that swept against the overhanging eaves, attempered the cheery western
sunshine.'   I looked from the little northern
window whence the old pastor watched the
battle, and in the small dining-room beneath it,
upon the first floor, there were

"'Dainty chicken, snow-white bread,'

and the golden juices of Italian vineyards, which still feast insatiable memory.

"Our author occupied the Old Manse for three years. During that time he was not seen, probably, by more than a dozen of the villagers. His walks could easily avoid the town, and upon the river he was always sure of solitude. It was his favorite habit to bathe every evening in the river, after nightfall, and in that part of it over which the old bridge stood, at which the battle was fought. Sometimes, but rarely, his boat accompanied another up the stream, and I recall the silence and preternatural vigor with which, on one occasion, he wielded his paddle to counteract the bad rowing of a friend who conscientiously considered it his duty to do something and not let Hawthorne work alone, but who, with every stroke, neutralized all Hawthorne's efforts. I suppose he would have struggled until he fell senseless, rather than ask his friend to desist. His principle seemed to be, if a man cannot understand without talking to him, it is useless to talk, because it is immaterial whether such a man understands or not. His own sympathy was so broad and sure that, although nothing had been said for hours, his companion knew that nothing had escaped his eye, nor had a single pulse of beauty in the day or scene or society failed to thrill his heart. In this way his silence was most social. Everything seemed to have

been said. It was a Barmecide feast of discourse
from which a greater satisfaction resulted than
from an actual banquet.

"When a formal attempt was made to desert
this style of conversation, the result was ludicrous. Once Emerson and Thoreau arrived to
pay a call. They were shown into the little parlor upon the avenue, and Hawthorne presently
entered. Each of the guests sat upright in his
chair like a Roman senator. 'To them,' Hawthorne, like a Dacian King. The call went on,
but in a most melancholy manner. The host sat
perfectly still, or occasionally propounded a question which Thoreau answered accurately, and
there the thread broke short off. Emerson delivered sentences that only needed the setting of
an essay to charm the world; but the whole visit
was a vague ghost of the Monday Evening Club
at Mr. Emerson's—it was a great failure. Had
they all been lying idly on the river brink or
strolling in Thoreau's blackberry pastures, the
result would have been utterly different. But
imprisoned in the proprieties of a parlor, each a
wild man in his way, with a necessity of talking
inherent in the nature of the occasion, there was
only a waste of treasure. This was the only 'call'
in which I ever knew Hawthorne to be involved.

"In Mr. Emerson's house I said it seemed always morning. But Hawthorne's black-ash trees
and scraggy apple boughs shaded

"'A land in which it seemed always afternoon.'

I do not doubt that the lotus grew along the grassy marge of the Concord behind his house, and that it was served, subtly concealed, to all his guests. The house, its inmates, and its life lay dream-like upon the edge of the little village. You fancy that they all came together and belonged together, and were glad that at length some idol of your imagination, some poet whose spell had held you, and would hold you forever, was housed as such a poet should be.

"During the lapse of the three years since the bridal tour of twenty miles ended at the 'two tall gate - posts of roughhewn stone,' a little wicker wagon had appeared at intervals upon the avenue, and a placid babe, whose eyes the soft Concord day had touched with the blue of its beauty, lay looking tranquilly up at the grave old trees, which sighed lofty lullabies over her sleep. The tranquillity of the golden-haired Una was the living and breathing type of the dreamy life of the Old Manse. Perhaps, that being attained, it was as well to go. Perhaps our author was not surprised or displeased when the hints came, 'growing more and more distinct, that the owner of the old house was pining for his native air.' One afternoon I entered the study and learned from its occupant that the last story he should ever write there was written."

BROOK FARM AND CONCORD

In the midnight chapter of his "Blithedale Romance," Hawthorne described an incident which actually took place in Concord. A young girl drowned herself, and her body was found as there set forth. Hawthorne wrote a full account of the drowning in his journal, which is printed by Julian Hawthorne in his biography of "Nathaniel Hawthorne and His Wife." No mention is made of Curtis, who took part in the search, and who gave his own account of the affair in his paper on Hawthorne. When Thoreau went to New York, in 1843, he put his boat into the keeping of Curtis, and he and Channing made their excursions on the river in it. In it they searched for Mary Hunt, who lived near Channing. Curtis's account of this affair deserves to be placed by the side of Hawthorne's:

"Martha was the daughter of a plain Concord farmer, a girl of delicate and shy temperament, who excelled so much in study that she was sent to a fine academy in a neighboring town, and won all the honors of the course. She met at the school and in the society of the place a refinement and cultivation, a social gayety and grace, which were entirely unknown in the hard life she had led at home, and which by their very novelty, as well as because they harmonized with her own nature and dreams, were doubly beautiful and fascinating. She enjoyed this life to the full, while her timidity kept her only a spectator; and she ornamented it with a fresher grace, suggestive of the woods and fields, when she ventured to engage in the airy game. It was a sphere for her capacities and talents. She shone in it, and the consciousness of a true position and genial appreciation gave her the full use of all her powers. She admired and was admired. She was surrounded by gratifications of taste, by the stimulants and rewards of ambition. The world was happy, and she was worthy to live in it. But at times a cloud suddenly dashed athwart the sun —a shadow stole, dark and chill, to the very edge of the charmed circle in which she stood. She knew well what it was, and what it foretold, but she would not pause nor heed. The sun shone again, the future smiled; youth, beauty, and all hopes and thoughts bathed the moment in lambent light.

"But school-days ended at last, and with the receding town in which they had been passed, the bright days of life disappeared, and forever. It was probable that the girl's fancy had been fed, perhaps indiscreetly pampered, by her experience there. But it was no fairy-land. It was an academy town in New England, and the fact that it was so alluring is a fair indication of the kind of life from which she had emerged, and to which she now returned. What could she do? In the dreary round of petty details, in the incessant drudgery of a poor farmer's household,

with no companions or any sympathy—for the
family of a hard-working New-England farmer
are not the Chloes and Clarissas of pastoral
poetry, nor the cowboys Corydons — with no
opportunity of retirement and cultivation, for
reading and studying—which is always voted
'stuff' under such circumstances—the light suddenly quenches out of life, what was she to do?

"The simple answer is that she had only used
all her opportunities, and that, although it was
no fault of hers that the routine of her life was in
every way repulsive, she did struggle to accom-
modate herself to it, and failed. When she
found it impossible to drag on at home, she became an inmate of a refined and cultivated
household in the village, where she had opportunity to follow her own fancies and to associate
with educated and attractive persons. But even
here she could not escape the feeling that it was
all temporary, that her position was one of de-
pendence; and her pride, now grown morbid,
often drove her from the very society which
alone was agreeable to her. This was all genuine. There was not the slightest strain of the
femme incomprise in her demeanor. She was always shy and silent, with a touching reserve
which won interest and confidence, but left also
a vague sadness in the mind of the observer.
After a few months she made another effort to
rend the cloud which was gradually darkening

around her, and opened a school for young children. But although the interest of friends secured her a partial success, her gravity and sadness failed to excite the sympathy of her pupils, who missed in her the playful gayety always most winning to children. Martha, however, pushed bravely on, a figure of tragic sobriety to all who watched her course. The farmers thought her a strange girl, and wondered at the ways of the farmer's daughter who was not content to milk cows and churn butter and fry pork, without further hope or thought. The good clergyman of the town, interested in her situation, sought a confidence she did not care to bestow, and so, doling out a, b, c to a wild group of boys and girls, she found that she could not untie the Gordian knot of her life, and felt with terror that it must be cut.

"One summer evening she left her father's house and walked into the fields alone. Night came, but Martha did not return. The family became anxious, inquired if any one had noticed the direction in which she went, learned from the neighbors that she was not visiting, that there was no lecture nor meeting to detain her, and wonder passed into apprehension. Neighbors went into the adjacent woods and called, but received no answer. Every instant the awful shadow of some dread event solemnized the gathering groups. Every one thought what no one dared whisper, until a low voice suggested the river. Then with the swiftness of certainty all friends far and near were roused, and thronged along the banks of the stream. Torches flashed in the boats that put off in the terrible search. Hawthorne, then living in the Old Manse, was summoned, and the man whom the villagers had only seen at morning as a musing spectre in his garden, now appeared among them at night, to devote his strong arm and steady heart to their service. The boats drifted slowly down the stream, the torches flashed strangely upon the black repose of the waters, and upon the long slim grasses that weeping fringed the marge. Upon both banks silent and awe-stricken crowds hastened along, eager and dreading to find the slightest trace of what they sought. Suddenly they came to a few articles of dress, heavy with the night dew. No one spoke, for no one had doubted the result. It was clear that Martha had strayed to the river, and quietly asked of its stillness the repose she sought. The boats gathered around the spot. With every implement that could be of service the melancholy search began. Long intervals of fearful silence ensued, but at length, towards midnight, the sweet face of the dead girl was raised more placidly to the stars than ever it had been to the sun.

"So ended a village tragedy. The reader may possibly find in it the original of the thrilling conclusion of the 'Blithedale Romance,' and learn anew that dark as is the thread with which Hawthorne weaves his spells, it is no darker than those with which tragedies are spun, even in regions apparently so torpid as Concord."

Far too much has been made of the realistic elements in the "Blithedale Romance." Hawthorne says in his preface that " he has occasionally availed himself of his actual reminiscences;" but it cannot be claimed that he did anything more. The fact seems to be that he used such reminiscences and incidents merely as stimuli to his imagination, that the real romance of the story was purely of his own creation. So far as he used the facts of his life at Brook Farm it was to give an air of reality to his story ; and in no other sense can it be accepted as truthful to Brook Farm life. For instance, his Zenobia was in every sense an original creation, and not a description of any person he had known. Three persons he knew at Brook Farm gave him hints, traits of character, and points of departure for the activity of his imagination. The stately elements in Zenobia resembled those of Mrs. George Ripley, her luxurious tastes were like those of Mrs. Almira Barlow, while her genius and brilliancy had a few similarities to Margaret Fuller. His habit seems to have been to take a single incident in the life of a person, and to make that the chief one in a character. In this way his romances gained a realistic phase of a very impressive kind; but the character of a person as a whole he never copied. It is a strange comment on his powerful writing that so much should have been made of his superficial realism, while the persistent and profound romanticism of his work is too often overlooked. Yet this was one of the weird results of his genius, that his imagination weaves for itself a world more real than life itself, and that claims for itself an acceptance as truer to facts than the word of the historian.

In his paper on Emerson, Curtis gives further account of his life in Concord. He said that "Thoreau lives in the berry-pastures upon a bank over Walden Pond, and in a little house of his own building. One pleasant summer afternoon a small party of us helped him raise it—a bit of life as Arcadian as any at Brook Farm. Elsewhere in the village he turns up arrow-heads abundantly, and Hawthorne mentions that Thoreau initiated him into the mystery of finding them." His account of the club which gathered for a few evenings in Emerson's study deserves to be placed here in order to complete his story of Concord experiences, the fictitious names used by him being changed to the real ones:

"It was in the year 1845 that a circle of persons of various ages, and differing very much in everything but sympathy, found themselves in Concord. Towards the end of the autumn, Mr. Emerson suggested that they should meet every Monday evening through the winter in his library. 'Monsieur Aubépine,' 'Miles Coverdale,' and other phantoms, since known as Nathaniel Hawthorne, who then occupied the Old Manse; the inflexible Henry Thoreau, a scholastic and pastoral Orson, then living among the blackberry pastures of Walden Pond; Plato Skimpole [Margaret Fuller's name for Alcott], then sublimely meditating impossible summer-houses in a little house on the Boston Road; the enthusiastic agriculturist and Brook Farmer [George Bradford], then an inmate of Mr. Emerson's house, who added the genial cultivation of a scholar to the amenities of the natural gentleman; a sturdy farmer-neighbor [Edmund Hosmer], who had bravely fought his weary way through inherited embarrassment to the small success of a New England husbandman; two city youths [George and Burrill Curtis], ready for the fragments from the feast of wit and wisdom; and the host himself, composed the club. Ellery Channing, who had that winter harnessed his Pegasus to the New York *Tribune*, was a kind of corresponding member. The news of this world was to be transmitted through his eminently practical genius, as the club deemed itself competent to take charge of tidings from all other spheres.

"I went the first evening very much as Ixion may have gone to his banquet. The philosophers sat dignified and erect. There was a constrained but very amiable silence, which had the impertinence of a tacit inquiry, seeming to ask, 'Who will now proceed to say the finest thing that has ever been said?' It was quite involuntary and unavoidable, for the members lacked that fluent social genius without which a club is impossible. It was a congress of oracles on the one hand, and of curious listeners upon the other. I vaguely remember that the Orphic Alcott invaded the Sahara of silence with a solemn 'Saying,' to which, after due pause, the honorable member for Blackberry Pastures responded by some keen and graphic observations, while the Olympian host, anxious that so much material should be spun into something, beamed smiling encouragement upon all parties. But the conversation became more and more staccato. Hawthorne, a statue of night and silence, sat a little removed, under a portrait of Dante, gazing imperturbably upon the group; and as he sat in the shadow, his dark hair and eyes and suit of sables made him, in that society, the black thread of mystery which he weaves into his stories; while the shifting presence of the Brook Farmer played like heat lightning around the room.

"I remember little else but a grave eating of

russet apples by the erect philosophers, and a solemn disappearance into night. The club struggled through three Monday evenings. Alcott was perpetually putting apples of gold in pictures of silver; for such was the rich ore of his thoughts coined by the deep melody of his voice. Thoreau charmed us with the secrets won from his interviews with Pan in the Walden woods; while Emerson, with the zeal of an engineer trying to dam wild waters, sought to bind the wide-flying embroidery of discourse into a whole of clear, sweet sense. But still in vain. The oracular sayings were the unalloyed saccharine element; and every chemist knows how much else goes to practical food—how much coarse, rough, woody fibre is essential. The club struggled on valiantly, discoursing celestially, eating apples, and disappearing in the dark, until the third evening it vanished altogether. But I have since known clubs of fifty times the number, whose collected genius was not more than that of either of the Dii Majores of our Concord coterie. The fault was its too great concentration. It was not relaxation, as a club should be, but tension. Society is a play, a game, a tournament; not a battle. It is the easy grace of undress; not an intellectual, full-dress parade."

VII

As will have been seen, Curtis never lost his interest in Brook Farm or his faith in the principles on which it was founded. In his letters to Dwight he clearly pointed out its defects, and he indicated in an emphatic manner that he could not accept some of its methods. He showed that he was an individualist rather than an associationist or socialist, that his supreme faith was in individual effort, and in each person making himself right before he undertook to reform society. His "Easy Chair" essays make it clear that he saw with keen vision the limitations of Brook Farm; but it had for him a distinct charm, and one that increased rather than grew less as the years went on. The Brook Farm effort to right the wrongs of society, to give all persons an opportunity in life, and to bring the help of all to the aid of each one, he heartily accepted in its spirit and intent; and to that faith he ever held with unswerving confidence.

Not less did the Concord episode remain with Curtis as a bright spot in his life. He gladly went to Concord whenever the opportunity offered; he frequently lectured there, and was always heard with delight; and he gave the Centennial Address, April 19, 1875, on the occasion of the one hundredth anniversary of the battle at the old north bridge.

It was a part of the Brook Farm and Concord life which Curtis continued in his intimacy with Dwight. So great was the confidence of this friendship that he wrote to Dwight as soon as his marriage had been arranged, telling him of his happiness, and telling him that the promised bride was the daughter of their old Brook Farm friends, the Francis George Shaws. "Do you remember her in Brook Farm days?" he asked. "There was never anything that made parents and children happier." In closing his letter he wrote: "When do you come to New York? I so want you to see her and know her; then of course you will love her. Give my love to your wife—think that love is not for this world, but forever!—and remember your friend who remembers you." In his reply, Dwight said:

"You are right, George; link your destinies with *youth*. I scarcely believe in anything else —except Spring and Morning. But then, there is a way of making these—the soul of them— perpetual; and you have the secret of it, I am sure, better than most of us.

"To think of that child, who used to play about Brook Farm, and go through finger drudg- ery under my piano-professorship (Heaven save the mark!), the child of our young friends, Mr. and Mrs. F. S. (how can you think of them as parents?) being the future Mrs. Howadji! or I a dull drudge of an editor! I do wish indeed to see and know her, and doubt not I shall find your glowing statements all confirmed, and that in your height of joy you need not be ashamed to ' blush it east and blush it west.' There is a certain ' Maud '-like ecstasy in your note that makes me think of that.

"A small bird had already sung the news in my ear. But it was doubly pleasant to have it straight from you. It was good in you to remember me so. . . . Would that I might see you in New York! but I must content myself with the not very remote prospect of having you by the hand here. Till then, believe me happy in your happiness, and faithfully as ever your friend."

Francis George Shaw, and his wife Sarah B. Shaw, were not members of the Brook Farm community; but they lived in the immediate vicinity, often visited the farm, joined in its entertainments, and were intimate friends of the leaders of the association. He was a contributor to the *Harbinger*, for which he wrote a number of articles in favor of the associationist social movement. He made an admirable translation of George Sand's "Consuelo" for the paper, in which that novel was for the first time printed in this country. Their children were frequently at the farm, and grew up in the midst of such ideas and influences as it fostered. One of them was that Colonel Robert G. Shaw who was "buried with his niggers" at Fort Wagner, after having led one of the most gallant military movements of modern times. Three of the daughters married, Curtis, General Barlow, and General Charles Russell Lowell. Mrs. Josephine Shaw Lowell has made for herself a lasting name by her philanthropies, and her generous interest in all good causes. Mrs. Shaw wrote the biography of her son Robert, which was published in the work devoted to the Harvard graduates who fell in the Civil War.

The real effect of Brook Farm, and that movement of which it was a part, can be rightly understood only when there is taken into consideration what they did for such persons as Shaw, Curtis, Barlow, Lowell, and Mrs. Lowell. These persons were trained by Brook Farm and Transcendentalism; and their aspirations, philanthropies, chivalrous spirit, and romantic courage were fostered and developed by them. The tone and quality of Shaw's courage, and of his heroic effort for the colored men, found in Brook Farm their motive and incentive; and in Brook Farm because it represented a phase of life much larger than itself, one that fosters the noblest faith in men and in the spiritual future of humanity. Of Barlow and Lowell it may be also said that their heroism and their patriotism were the legitimate products of that movement whose hope and faith were the inspiration of their youth. To this source was due Barlow's love of justice, his unflinching courage in opposing self-seekers and partisan patriots, and his trust in the ultimate worth of what is right and true.

The letters printed in this volume have a large interest as indications of how George William Curtis was making ready for his life-work. His independence, his love of humanity, his courage in maintaining his own convictions, his chivalrous and romantic spirit, his literary skill and charm, his profound spiritual convictions, that would not be limited by any sectarian bounds, all find expression here in such form as to give sure promise for his future. It was a somewhat erratic kind of training which Curtis received; but for him it was better than any college of his day could have given him. Admirably fitted to his tastes, it was no less well adapted to his needs. It fostered in him all that was best in his character, and it served to bring out his genius to its rounded expression.

The two years which Curtis spent in Concord must have been of the greatest value to him. His contact with Emerson was of itself of inestimable worth, for it gave him that enthusiasm for ideas, that contact with a noble life lived for the highest ends of spiritual development, which fostered in him the enthusiasms which were so genuine a part of his life. Without Brook Farm, Transcendentalism, and Emerson, it is quite safe to say that the life of Curtis would have been less worthy of our admiration. The stay in Concord was a time of seed-planting, and the harvest came in all that the man was in later years. Without the enthusiasms then cherished the independent in politics would have been less courageous. And these letters may suggest anew one of the most important lessons of education, that without enthusiasms no man can do any great or noble work in the world. What will give to youth visions, ideals, and enthusiasms is worth all other parts of culture, for out of these grow the noblest results of human willing, thinking, and doing.

EARLY LETTERS TO JOHN S. DWIGHT

EARLY LETTERS TO JOHN S. DWIGHT

I

Are you quite recovered from those divine enchantments which held us bound so long? Memory preserves for me those silvery sounds, and almost I seem to catch their echo. Have we indeed heard the Siren song—are we un- scathed? Let me be your Father John, and to these reverend years commit the tale of youth- ful fervor. So good a Catholic as I, of course, has long ago made confession. But another yet remains for me—namely, that I cannot get that song. Yesterday I heard from Isaac, who can- not buy it in New York. Nothing but a copy for the guitar and that Rosalie. Would it be an expensive thing to import? Reed told me he could do that, but as I supposed there was no doubt of its being in New York, I said nothing about it. She should have the song; it would be so fine falling out of her mouth. Mouth-dropped gems would be no longer a fable. As, indeed, we have seen already. For what so universal an Interpreter as music? That art has the gift of tongues (*ecce*, the Singing-School).

Burrill met with a mishap on Wednesday. We were walking out of town, and he, springing from a wall, turned his ankle and sprained it. He is therefore laid up for some days. It is a disappointment to him, for he hoped to leave on Monday next, and meanwhile see several persons. I doubt if he can step on his foot so soon.

I had yesterday a German letter from Isaac; German in spirit, not in language. He has certainly a great heart, more delicate in his character than I thought, with a constant force, nervous, not muscular strength.

Will you accept so city-like a letter? I am busy or I should write more; another time will suffice. Let me accept from you a country-like letter. Yours in the bonds,

G. W. C.

II

PROVIDENCE, *September* 1, 1843.

MY DEAR FRIEND, — Your letter did not reach my hands until last evening, when I returned from Newport, where I have passed the last eight days, how pleasantly I need not tell you. After the quiet beauty of our farm home, there was a striking grandeur in the sea that I never beheld so plainly before. There is something sublimely cheerful about the ocean, altho' it is so stored with woe, and so constantly suggestive it is of that ocean, life, whereon we all float.

It was pleasant to me that Nature confirmed my judgment of Tennyson. The little poem that closes one of the volumes, "Break, break, break," etc., is so exquisitely human and tender, with all its vague and dim beauty, that the waves dashed to its music, and silently the whole sea sung the song. Just so the jottings down of poets, the few words that must be said, tho' the Nature which they sing is so limitless, and inexpressible are the blossoms of poetry and all literature. Will not the little song of Shakespeare's, "Take, oh! take those lips away," be as immortal as Hamlet? Not because chance may print them together, but because it is as universal and more delicate an expression. That charm pervades our favorite, Tennyson. There is no rough-marked outline, all fades away upon earnest contemplation into the tones of his songs, into the colors of the sky. So in the landscape, tint fades gently into tint, and the beauty that attracts spreads from leaf to hill, from hill to horizon, till the whole is bathed in sunlight. Is not this fact also recognized in other arts? In painting, the great picture is without marked outline;

in music, the truest and deepest is undefined.
Beethoven is greater than Haydn. The precision which offends in manner is as disagreeable
everywhere else. Is it not because when named
as Precision, the depth which necessarily means
a graceful form is absent? As when we say a
woman has beautiful eyes we indirectly acknowledge her want of universal beauty. Certainly a man of elegant manners is admired not
for himself, but what he represents. Indeed, all
society is only thus endurable. Nature, and to
me particularly the ocean, makes no such partial impression; and therefore the poet who sits
nearest to the great heart sings rather the sense
of vague beauty and aspiration, of tender remembrance and gentle hope, than a bald description of the sight. The ocean is not fathomless
water nor the woods green trees to him, but a
presence, and a key that unlocks the chambers
of his soul where the diamonds are. Therefore,
when I have been into nearer conversation with
Nature I have little to say, but my life is deepened. The poet is he who with deepened life
chants also a flowing hymn which utters the
music of that life. You will understand why
the little poem seems to me so fine, therefore.
This water I also see; but not in me lies the
power of the due expression of its influence.

There was another pleasant aspect in Newport, of persons. I walked one evening towards

the town (for I was boarding in the outskirts), and passed an encampment of soldiers, who in their gay uniforms glittered among the lighted tents like soldier fays. The band in the shadow of the camp was playing very sweetly airs proper for that fading light, half-mournful, half-tender and hopeful. I passed by the houses brilliantly lighted and filled with finely dressed people, who also thronged the streets. Before one of the principal hotels was a band from the fort serenading, and surrounded with a crowd of easy listeners. The ice-cream resort was filled, the cottages shone among the trees, and an air of entire abandonment to joy filled the place. Old men and young men, women and girls, seemed to have laid aside all business, all care, and to be only gay. It was a vision of the Lotos islands, an earthly portrait of that meek repose which haunts us ideally sometimes.

I was surprised upon my return to find Burrill still here. He is able only to crutch about the house, but will probably return to Brook Farm with me during the latter part of next week, which is the commencement week here . . .

I should have been glad to have seen the gay picnic, and to have heard the O.; let me hope she will not be gone when I return. I am exceedingly obliged for your kind suggestion of "Adelaide," and if you choose to present it as a joint gift, you confer a great pleasure upon me.

Commend me particularly to Almira; to the young men whom you will, including mainly Charles D. and James S.; to Mr. and Mrs. R.; and if you will write me again you will be sure that your proxy will be welcome to

Your friend,

G. W. CURTIS.

Will you say to Miss Russell that I shall see my aunt this afternoon, and will perform her commission. Moreover, that I am gratified at so distinguished a mark of her approbation as the permission to escort a plant to her garden.

G. W. C.

III

NEW YORK, *Saturday eve'g, November* 11, 1843.

Your letter has just reached me, my dear friend, loaded with much that was not in it, and which needed only a person or a letter from a region so delightful to bear it to me. Already my life at the Farm is removed and transfigured. It stands for so much in my experience, and is so fairly rounded, that I know the experience could never return, tho' the residence might be renewed. When we mend the broken chain, we see ever after the point of union.

To-night the wind sighs thro' the chimney, complaining and wailing and melting away in a depth of sadness, as if it would pacify its own sorrow, and found newer grief in that need: The clouds break and roll away in the sky, and the wan moon sails up as if to a weary duty. Yet so calm it is, so pure, that it chides weariness and preaches a deep, still hope. In the city I seem not to breathe quite freely yet, but daily I gain ground and air. It is so different, even more than I tho't; so new, tho' I had seen it for years; so full, tho' I walk miles without speaking or seeing a face seen before. I must constantly say to myself, "Be quiet, be quiet. This huge enigma will gradually explain itself, and out of these conventions and courtesies you shall see the same tender Nature looking that so enchanted your country life."

Here is Burrill, and we are of more worth to each other than ever before. Sometimes I fear to think how much. He was as glad to see me as the old Christians a prophet, for I know him best of all.

The aspect of things here impresses me mainly with the absolute necessity and duty of making our place good. The stern, stirring activity around me compels me to give account to myself of my silence and repose. The answer is always clear and steady. I have not heard the voice. Yet my mind begins to shape some outline of life. Of this I am assured, that in this world of work, where the hum of business makes music with the stars, I must work too. And how I must work, by what handle I shall grasp the world and justify my consumption of its food, that begins to appear. My Genius is not decided enough to lead me unquestioning in any one direction, and my taste is so equally cultivated and developed that choice seems somewhat arbitrary. Yet it is not so. Above all, I regret no culture, tho' it may have thus multiplied the roads to be chosen. It is a tinge and charm to whatever is performed.

A gentleman in never so ragged clothes is a gentleman still. You may be sure nothing has charmed me more than my meeting with Isaac in his mealy clothes and brown-paper cap. His manner had a grand dignity, because he was universally related by his diligent labor, and my conversation with him was as earnest and happy as any intercourse I have had with him. This general activity does not reprove me, for my silence respects itself and gives good reasons why judgment should not proceed. And therefore it views more lovingly what surrounds it. The God stirs within, and presently will say something. Let us plant ourselves there and be lawyers that we may so dispense justice, not that we may get bread; and priests, because the Divine will speaks thro' us; and merchants and doctors and shoemakers and bakers, from the same reason. If we honestly serve in any such profession, bread will come of course.

Your letter has quickened my thought upon these things, quite active before. My impulse is to say at once, go. The worst and all you can dread is the foul breath that will befog your fair name, because E. W. has done what he has, because you *were* a minister and *are* a Transcendentalist and a seceder from the holy office, and a dweller at *that place*, unknown to perfumed respectability and condemned of prejudice and error. This is the first great reason, and the second is not unlike unto it. It is that you retard your preparation for any permanent pursuit, as a centre of your sensuous life, by passing two or three years in Europe. With respect to the first reason, not your own feelings, but those of your friends, demand some consideration. In Heaven's court will their sorrow at your departure and intimacy with E. W. at this time outweigh your own happiness at the trip, and because so you lend your own good character to one perhaps unjustly condemned. Such a sudden departure and intimacy with him might have an indirect influence upon your future attempts to base yourself in some way. If your mind is determining itself towards no pursuit, and you anticipate the same general employment that has filled the last year or two, I should say go. If God doesn't call here, he may in Europe;

and if not for years, your voyage cannot inter-
fere with him. There are privater reasons, which
you know, of his character and of your proba-
bility of assimilation, and of your independence
in intimacies. Perhaps you may link little fingers, if you cannot clasp the whole hand. On
the whole, I should say go, though not without
due thought of friends, to whom your name
and relation may be more than your friendship.
You will soon let me know of your movements,
will you not?

For a week or two, I am man of the house
for my cousin, whose husband is in Boston.
Burrill fulfils the same duty for an aunt. It is
a great separation, though only a step separates
us when I am at home; but the fine social
sympathy of actual contact, in the early morning and late night, the kind deeds that link the
minutes and adorn the hours, the tender sweets
of the dignity of friendship without its form—
these are buds that bloom only in the warmth
of hands perpetually united.

To-night Charles Dana and Isaac and Burrill
came to see me. I smelled summer leaves and
heard summer flutes as I stood with them and
talked. Charles was never so important to me;
he was himself and all Brook Farm beside. We
are all going to hear William Henry Channing
in the morning. Last Sunday at the church door
I met C. P. Cranch and his wife. I mean to go

and see them very soon, though they live *streets* away. Of Isaac I have seen much for a week's space. He lives two miles or more from us.

I have heard no music yet. Max Böhrer concerts on Monday with Timm, Mrs. Sutton, Antogigni, and Schafenberg; I mean to go. The Philharmonic concerts begin a week from this evening. They have four concerts, and the subscription is $10, for which one obtains three tickets to each concert, and the privilege of buying two occasional tickets at $1 50 each. A singular arrangement. They are to play the 8th Symphony next Saturday. I know not what else.

Give Almira a great deal of love from me. I shall sing a song to her solitude and patiently await the response. I have begun to read "Wilhelm Meister" in German. I read about three or four hours a day, then an hour or two in Latin, and the rest to poetical reading—Beaumont and Fletcher, Ford, Massinger, Shakespeare, and the Bible, at present. In Worcester I found Montaigne, whom I devoured. What cheerful good sense! I have begun also to learn two or three of B.'s waltzes from note. "La Dobur" I have almost accomplished. Possibly I shall thus pick up some *note* knowledge, though I do not build any castles. Good-night. Could I but send myself in my letter!   Your friend,

G. W. C.

Tuesday morning. I concluded to retain my letter for Charles, who leaves to-day. Charles and Isaac and Burrill and I all went to Max Böhrer's concert last evening. The hall was full, 1000 or 1500 people present. I was glad to go, for he introduced me to the Instrument, but no more. He has great skill, and has fully mastered it. That is what persevering talent can always do. Böhrer loved his instrument because he could display himself by its aid, not because it was through his genius a minister and revealer of the art to himself and others. His conceit is sublime. It was entire and unique. His posture and air were ridiculously Olympian. Mrs. Sutton is very fat and has a thin voice. There are some good tones in it, but she undertakes the most difficult music. Antignini sings pleasantly but with great effort. All his songs were his own composition, and all Max Böhrer's his. In fact, it was not a musical festival so much as a gymnasium for musical instruments, both mechanical and human. Timm and Scharfenberg both played admirably. I saw Fred'k Rakemann in the crowd; could not conveniently speak to him, and am going, as soon as I can find out where he lives, to see him. His face was so sad that I wanted to go to him and say some tenderer word than I should have said had I spoken. Yet after all he doesn't need tender words, but a calm, grateful demeanor towards him.

JOHN S. DWIGHT

I wish that I could tell all the glories of my trip to New York. I went from Worcester over the Western R. R. to Albany and down the river. Some other day shall be consecrated to their fit celebration when the recollection may be pleasant and soothing among cares that disturb. Now I expect Charles every moment to go with me to see Cranch.

Ask Charles for all news about our "externe." Remember me most tenderly to my many friends at Brook Farm.

G. W. C.

IV

NEW YORK, *November* 20, '43.

Certainly, my dear Friend, the concert of the Philharmonic Society on Saturday evening was the finest concert ever given in the country. It is pleasant to see the homage paid to the art indirectly by the whole style of the concert. The room is small, holding 1000 people. Every gentleman goes in full-dress, and the ladies in half-dress. Various members of the society are appointed managers, distinguished by a ribboned button-hole, and they provide seats for the audience. No bills are issued before the night, so there are only rumors of what the *particular* will be, with a quiet consciousness that the *general* will be fine. So we arrived on Saturday evening and found the following bill: Symphony No. 7 in A minor (Beethoven); Cavatina from an opera of Nini's (Signora Castellan); Overture to "Zauberflöte" (Mozart); Cavatina from Donizetti (Signora Castellan); Overture to "The Jubilee" (Weber). I think we have not had many such concerts.

The symphony was interpreted upon the bills as a musical presentment of the mythological story of Orpheus and Eurydice. That did very well as a figure to represent it, but it was taken by the audience as a theme; and they all fixed their eyes upon the explanation, thereby to judge the symphony. It was grand, and full of his genius. It was another of those earnest, hopeless questionings of Destiny. The very first bars were full of this. It opens with a crash of the whole orchestra, determined and inexorable. Then follows a low deep wailing of the flutes and horns, full of tenderness, of aspiration, of subdued hope; and another crash of the whole, like a lightning flash, instantaneous and scathing the world, sweeps across the plaintiveness of the wind instruments and as instantly is gone. The sad inquiry continues, the determined Thunder of Fate drowns it constantly, and it is lost. Then it becomes more imperious and active, and the call upon the Invisible and the Unanswerable sounds on every side, rises to the top of the flutes, sinks to the lowest bases, appears now among the violins, now vanishes to the rest, until it has disciplined the whole, and the whole orchestra together thunders out the call. Then comes the adagio, where, as always, the mystery seems to be developing itself, where the earnest-seeking solemnly consecrates itself to success; and the minuet and finale conclude—the soaring, mocking, hellish laughter of fiends and demons of the air, at baffled curiosity and blighted hope. Is not that what these symphonies express? The pith of the matter is never reached. The very movement of the adagio, while it expresses a deep, solemn hope, seems to mourn with unutterable sorrow that the hope must be only consecrated and profound, never realized. The climax of the music and the sentiment seems to be always in the adagio.

What remained for such a man as he, separate from all others and alone with his life, but to question the Fate that impelled him, now in this tone and now in that? What remained for such unsatisfied, joyless strength but the stern, wild laughter of fiends that the question could not be answered—and the deep wail of Fate, which also is sung in his music, that such strength should have the ruggedness of endurance but not the gracefulness of Faith? How I wished you had been there!

Castellan's voice is full and rich; it was very sweet, and she sang with warmth but no passion. She needs some cultivation yet, for her shake is not good. Why did we not hear Malibran? who was also so great an actor that she would have been famous without a voice. I could not for a moment suffer my idea of her to be compared with Castellan. Malibran must have been so lovely from her sensibility and passion, so commanding from the majesty of her voice, that the art and not the woman must have found newer worshippers with every new audience.

I hope to hear Cinto Damoreau this week. You have heard "The Magic Flute" overture, I think, so fairy-like and graceful, full of tender shadows and heart-rejoicing sunlight and aërial shapes that fade and glint like stars. And the magnificent "Jubilee" concluded with "God save the King."

Evening. My aunt sent for me to hear Timm play the "Pathetique." His playing is wonderfully graceful, his touch more delicate than either of the R.'s. But he lacks genius; and time and practice will give Fred. R. all that Timm has. He is very enthusiastic. I spoke to him of "Egmont;" he seemed delighted, said he hadn't heard it for 12 years, but instantly sat down and played portions of it. He promised to play the adagio of the "Pathetique" on the organ next Sunday. We had but a few moments, for his time is all devoted to teaching, or I should have kept him till midnight. He is so simple and natural about the matter that it is very pleasant to be with him. If you mention anything to him, he instantly runs to the piano and plays something from it. Imagine him the other evening standing up straddling the stool, a roll of music under each arm, gloves in hand, and playing a movement from one of the symphonies!

I have been to see Cranch; found his wife at home, whom I have not seen since January. They are pleasantly situated, though a good way off. He has a room in the house where he paints. I saw two of his landscapes, views from nature, that were very striking. If I should find fault, I should say they were too warmly colored; and I suspect that is his error, if he has any, from what his wife told me he said of one of Durand's.

Mr. Furness preached finely for us on Sunday. Mr. Dewey does not charm me at all. Have heard W. H. C. once, as Charles will have told you. Have not yet seen him, for I have been out to see people hardly at all. Met Isaac at the Saturday concert. He looks fresh and well. Seems better every way than I ever knew him. Has he not found his place? I must see him again to discern the direction of Almira, to whom I have a letter written partly, and know not how to address it.

Are you singing Eastward ho! or do you remain? Remember that he who criticises Handel and Mozart, as the " Democratic " witnesseth, owes something to the art—shall I say *his life ?* What literary work are you about, or have you still the same reluctance to assume the pen that you had? Let the consideration that the pen is so invaluable a minister to friendship tempt you to honor it more by use.

I have squeezed myself into such little space that I must defer an outline of my days till I write again. One moral inquiry for your wits, and I will withdraw into silence and the infinite. Does not one friend who indites many letters, unanswered, to another, thereby heap coals of fire upon somebody's head as effectually as if he fed the hungry? Scatter my love as broadly as you think it will bear, and reserve the carver's share for yourself.

G. W. C.

V

Saturday night, November 25, '43.

Why do I love music enough to be only a lover, and cannot offer it a life-devoted service? Yet the lover serves in his sort, and if I may not minister to it, it cannot fail to dignify and ennoble my life. I am just from hearing Ole Bull, who this evening made his first appearance in America. How shall I fitly speak to you of

him, how can I now, while the new vision of
beauty that he caused to sweep by still lingers?
Yet itself shall inspire me. The presence of so
noble a man allures to light whatever nobility
lies in us.

He came forward to a house crowded in every part with the calm simplicity of Genius.
There was no grimace, no graces, but a fine
grace that adorned his presence and assured one
that nothing could disappoint — that the simplicity of the man was the seal and crown of his
genius. A fair-haired, robust, finely formed
man, the full bloom of health shining on his
face, he appeared as the master of the great instrument, as the successor, in point of time, of
the world-famous Paganini. Yet was one confident that here was no imitator, but a pupil who
had sat thoughtfully at the master's feet and felt
that beneath the depth of his expression there
was yet a lower depth, who knew himself consecrated by a will grander than his will to the
service of an art so divine and so loved. In him
there was that sure prophecy of latent power
which surrounds genius, and assures us that the
thing done is an echo only and shadow of the
possible performance.

The playing followed this simple, majestic
appearance. It was full of music, irregular, wild,
yearning, trembling. His violin lay upon his
arm tenderly as a living thing; and such rich,

mellow, silver, shining tones followed his motion that one seemed to catch echoes of that eternal melody whereof music itself is but the shadow and presentment. The adagios reminded me of Beethoven, not as they were imitated, but as all the great ones, in their appearing, summon all the rest. The mechanical execution was faultless. I detected no thick note. It was smooth as the sea of summer, embosoming only deep cloud-shadows and the full sunlight, but no lesser thing. Then he came, and he withdrew; and my heart followed him.

Do not be alarmed if the critics call him cold, and speak of him disparagingly when others are mentioned. The noble and heroes serve divine powers, and at last win men. Men of talent and application love their instrument as it introduces the world to them; men of genius as it interprets to them and to the world the mystery of music. Genius men must reverence, and they are not apt to do it boisterously. Is not the influence of fine character, which is only genius for virtue, like the brooding of God over chaos? Which is chaos only to the blind, but teems with generous, melodious laws to the spiritually discerned. Creation is the opening of eyes, not the fabrication of objects. "Let there be light" is the creative fiat, spoken by every God-filled soul. Yet how sure is this power of Genius.

The world henceforth gives to Ole Bull the full and generous satisfaction of his needs. It cannot fail to esteem God's messengers when they come, if they be true and collected. Talent wins the same subsistence; earnest, unfailing, unshrinking endeavor wins it anywhere; but what does Talent and Trial do but imitate the action of the result of Genius! How sublime the revelations it makes in this art! While the rest have risen and culminated and paused, this seeks a zenith ever loftier and diviner. That deep nature, that central beauty, which all art strives to reveal, floats to us in these fine harmonies, to me more subtly and surely than elsewhere. But in this region, where my thought bears me, they are all united. This soft, silent face of Urania, which looks upon me sleeplessly and untired, is not its wonderful influence woven of that same essence that has ravished me to-night in the tones of the violin? In the coolness of thought, do not the masters of song, of painting, of sculpture meet in eternal congress, for in each is the appearance of equal skill? Raphael could have sung as Shakespeare, and Milton have hewn these massy forms as Angelo. Yet a divine economy rules these upper spiritual regions, as sure and steadfast as the order of the stars. Raphael must paint and Homer sing, yet the same soul gilds the picture and sweetens the song. So Venus and Mars shine yellow and red, but the same central fire is the light of each. In the capacity of doing all things well lies the willingness to serve one duty. The Jack of all trades is sure to be good at none, for who is good at all is Jack of one only. It seemed a bitter thing to me, formerly, that painters must only paint and sculptors carve; but I see now the wisdom. In one thing well done lies the secret of doing all.

Music, painting, are labels that designate the form of action; the soul of it lies below. The earnest merchant and the earnest anti-tradesman do join hands and work together. Not ends are demanded of them, but vital strength and soul. The world does not need that I name my work, but that the work be accomplished.

The midnight warns me to pause. The stillness accords with the intercourse of friendship, as the silence of space with the calm, speechless recognition of the planets. Thoughts of all friends circle round me like gentle breezes from the black wing of the night. Friends are equal and noble always to friends. Lovers only know the depths and the heights of lovers. Love prophesies only a surer, diviner friendship, crowned with the dignity and composure of God.

I shall re-enter the world through the white gate of dreams, yet more quiet and resolved that I have heard this man, more tender, more tolerant. He has touched strings of that harp whose vibrations never cease, but affirm the infiniteness of our being and its present habitation in Eternity.   Your friend,

G. W. C.

Wednesday.   Sunday P. M. I passed with Fred. Rakemann.   He was very glad to see me, and I him.   His fine face lighted with enthusiasm as we spoke of music, of Germany and its poets.   He played magnificently, among others "Adelaide," translated for the piano by Liszt, a beautiful andante of Chopin, some of Henselt, etc., until it was quite twilight.   Then I went away.   He promised to come and see me, nor shall I fail to see him as often as I think he will endure, though his days are so busy with teaching that I do not hope to find him except on Sundays.

To-night Ole Bull plays the second time.   I shall go to hear him.   The Frenchmen are cliqued against him, for Vieuxtemps has arrived, and they mean to maintain his superiority.   He has no announcement as yet.   My letter I will not close until to-morrow, and say a final word about Ole Bull.   Wednesday night.   I have heard him again, and the impression he made on Saturday is only deepened.   He played an adagio of Mozart's.   It was simple and severely chaste.   His beautiful simplicity is just the character to apprehend the delicate touches of the Master, which he drew to us, without any ornament or addition. It was as if Mozart had been in spirit in the instrument, and given us, with all the freshness of creation, the music that can never lose its bloom. Scharfenberg was in the box with us, Fred. Rakemann in the next box. I saw Castellan in a private box, and Isaac H. The evening was glorious. Had you only been there! Yet you will see him in Boston. Do not fail to write me how he impresses you— that is, particularly. I cannot misapprehend his power so much as not to feel that it will seem to you very grand. Observe his manner towards the orchestra, how Olympian, how supreme, yet with all the gentle grace and tenderness of pow- er! Good - night. May you ever hear sweet music!

VI

N. Y. *Friday, Dec.* 15, 1843.

Truly the musical art culminates in our ze- nith this winter. It gives me other thoughts than of music only, unfolds to me something more of art, and I am charmed constantly to see how calmly we receive the great artists, after the noise of their entry, as the world quietly accepts the light of stars and swings unastonished on its wonderful way. Ole Bull and the rest are the scouts we have sent on before us, and they return to tell us of the Wonderful Land, and bring mementos and captives from the rich Eldorado of our hopes. That country to which nature points, of which all art is the flaming beacon, and which the weary voyager home-returning from fruitless search tells us is in ourselves—not the less far away for that.

Ole Bull's quiet, rapt manner is the full remembrance of that land which he has seen, and which he unfolds to us—is always the character and expression of the deepest insight. Just look at our bill for the week which ends to-night: Monday, Vieuxtemps; Tuesday, Artot and Damoreau; Wednesday, Ole Bull, Miss Sperty (the new pianist), and Madame Sphor Zahn; Thursday, Castellan, Antoquin Brough and Sphor Zahn in the "Stabat Mater," followed by the "Battle of Waterloo Symphony," by Beethoven; Friday, Vieuxtemps again! Monday evening I could not hear Vieuxtemps, but went on Tuesday to hear C. Damoreau and Artot. The former, with the smallest voice, sings pleasantly from her wonderful cultivation, of which, however, the technicalities, so to say, are too much obtruded. She shakes through all her songs, and this power, which would render her plain singing so sure and pleasing, demands attention for itself, not because it improves the tone of the singing.

Artot is an elegant artist. He plays very finely, wonderfully; but the greater his execution the more marked appeared to me the difference between the highest cultivated talent and the supremacy of Genius. He played difficult music, he shook and warbled and imitated, some of his tones were very exquisite, but it was all lifeless, the passionless semblance of beauty. I was as if walking in a Gorgon's ice-palace, with magnificent, clear crystals, and noble, transparent pillars, and all the artifice of beauty and comfort, but evermore a deep chill from the lavish elegance. When he had done, I knew he had done his utmost, that he had exhausted hope. In him I found none of that depthless background which genius ever offers. He made sing in my ears the old text, "The things seen are temporal; the things unseen are eternal." His performance is a thing seen, not a dim beacon on the outskirts of an unexplored country, wherein we hear birds singing and rivers flowing, and see the great cloud-shadows fall upon the hills, where in the dim distance stately palaces are faintly traced, and the depthless woods fringe unknown seas. Artot's playing seemed to me like the full flower exhausting the plant; Ole Bull's like a star shining out of the infinite space.

Flowers wither, but the stars do not fade. We gather the blossoms with joy and hurry home; but the stars light us on our way and make our homes beautiful. Talent has something familiar and social in its impression and greeting; but Genius receives us with a calm dignity that transfigures courtesy and complaisance, and makes our relations healthy and grand. The whole tone of Artot's violin differs from Bull's. I felt they must not be compared, and so listened delightedly, but with a pale, ghastly joy. When I heard Ole, I could not sleep. It was like a fire shining out of heaven, sudden and bright. It kindled within me flames which seek heaven, disturbed the surface of my soul, evoking spirits out of that depth I did not know were there, and it was as if a thousand hopes, which were the substance and object of memory, rose out of their graves and held long vigil with me in those silent hours. How few of us can keep our balance when a regal soul dashes by. I presently recover myself, and serve with a milder and firmer persistence my own nature. The way is made clearer by these bright lights, universal nature shines fairer that there are so many single stars; but they must only be stars in my heaven and fires upon my hearth, nor burn out my heart by inserting themselves in my bosom.

The next night I went to hear Ole Bull again at the Tabernacle, which holds 3000 persons. The doors were open at 6, the concert began at 8. At quarter-past 6 the house was full, and at

7 was jammed, and hundreds went away. I arrived too late, but was so satisfied at the triumph that I went gladly home again, pleased to be one who could not hear.

Last evening I heard the "Stabat." Castellan has a magnificent voice. Does she not lack passion? She certainly needs cultivation. The symphony was merely a musical picture of the battle—a battle of Prague for the orchestra! It begins with a drum, a bugle-call follows; a march—and what march do you think? "Malbrook." Imagine me, a fervid worshipper of Beethoven, rushing in the crowd to hear a symphony wherein, with all orchestral force, the old song, L-a-w, Law, was banged into my ears. I sat in motionless dismay, while there followed another trumpeting and drumming and marching and imitations of musketry by some watchman's rattle. Then came some good passages, which confounded me only the more. Then, "God save the King," which announced the British victory. Anon followed some marches, with the occasional bang of the bass drum to "disfigure or present" the distant cannon; and then there was a pause, and the people began to get up. I was confounded, looked towards the orchestra, and they were moving away; and I discovered I had heard the whole—alas! the day. What it meant, what Beethoven meant by writing it, how he could be so purely external, how

134

he could so use the orchestra, I cannot comprehend. Perhaps it was a curious relaxation with
him, as artists imitate other instruments upon
their own—perhaps it is a joke—but that it was
a sad disappointment to me admits no perhaps.

Since the limitations of life appear most
forcibly to correspondents in limited sheets of
paper, let me bear away abruptly from music.
My German progresses finely. I have read
Novalis's poetry, and am just now finishing the
"Lehrjahre." I read three or four hours daily,
and am pleased at my progress. Burrill and I
have just finished Johnson's "Elements of Agricultural Chemistry" and Buel's book. I read to
him daily from Bunyan. I am also busy with
Beaumont and Fletcher, Paul's Epistles, and St.
Augustine. You will easily imagine that my
whole day is devoted to literature. After dinner, at 5 o'clock, I sally down Broadway for exercise; and in the evening, if I go to no concert,
usually seek my room and books. To-night, for
the first time, I am going out to a ball at a
friend's, the girl of whom you have heard me
speak as singing so well. Cranch I meet very
rarely. Have been only once to see him. W.
H. Channing do not yet know. At his meeting
I see Isaac and C. P. Cranch, and Rufus Dawes,
and Parke Godwin, William Chace, and a host of
the unconverted and heretical. Him I do not
yet know personally, nor Vathek. His enthusi-

astic manner, and the tranquil fervor of his character, charm me very much.

I find that I do not care to go after people. Perhaps I have been rather too much with them; at all events, I will go to see none for curiosity. Isaac is my good friend, and passed Sunday P.M. in my room. We spoke of the church and society, and all topics that do so excite the youthful mind. I must break short off to dress for my party. I shall speak to you again before you know that I have been.

Saturday. To-day I have finished the "Lehrjahre." It is very calm and wise. It is full of Goethe, and therefore leaves behind in its impression that almost indefinite want which his character leaves, a want apparently readily designated. Yet to say his intellect was disproportionately developed leaves us in doubt whether a pure natural growth of the moral nature would have harmonized with his peculiar manifestation of intellect. He is to me as a blind God, made wise by laborious experience, not perpetual sight. He is at least too large for the tip of a letter.

What do you read, or don't you read? Sunday. To-day I heard a fine sermon from W. H. Channing. There I met Isaac and C. P. Cranch. Walked home with the latter, who during the week had heard Ole Bull. I suppose he will write you of it. Prof. Adam, from Northampton, was there. At our church, a few Sundays since, I saw

Mrs. Delano, late Kate Lyman, and her sister
Susan. The latter was beautiful. She seemed
like a pure, passionless saint. Had I been in
a Catholic church I had imagined her to have
been some holy being, incarnated by her deep
sympathy with the worshippers. I hardly saw
her, just enough to receive a poetic impression.

How little I have said! My life is very quiet,
yet very full. Your letters are very grateful to
me. One dares trust so much more to paper
than to conversation. Friends living intimately
learn of each other from tones and glances, not
by conversation. Friends meet intellectually in
words, lovers heartfully in words.

Macready has gone and I did not see him;
he played nothing of Shakespeare. Shall I direct
to Brook Farm or Boston? More anon.

Yrs ever,

G. W. C.

VII

NEW YORK, Friday, Dec. 22, '43.

A merry Christmas to you, and to all Christian souls. How brave goes the year to its setting! These calm, cold days impress me like the
fine characters of history and the elder time, inspired with a generous wisdom, and prophesying
what shall be the newest and best word of hope
in our day. The season embraces and surpasses

those old men, even the finest. To-day, as I walked, the magnificence of the closing year, so steadfast and sure, sparing no sunshine nor rain, passing quietly out to be renewed nevermore, quite reproved the solemn martyrdoms of men, upon which we hang our hopes.

Nature is great that she does not suffer us to define her influence upon ourselves. Like all greatness, she suggests to us beauty and grace, not as attributes of hers, but fair buds and flowers of the soul. Therefore, in the full presence of nature, the grandest deeds seem harmonious and the wisdom of Plato, and actions whose greatness is the centre, not the utmost compression, of our life are harmonious and symmetrical. To the Greeks and Jews the Gospel is blindness and a stumbling-block, but joy and peace to the elect.

Nothing is so stern and lofty a cordial to me as this severe inscrutability of nature. I must obey or die, and dying is no help to me, for the spirit that rules now rules evermore. How like a god sits she brooding over the world, announcing her laws by blows and knocks, by agonies and convulsions, by the mouths of wise men, affirming that as the sowing so also is the harvest. And there is no alleviation, no palliation. She heeds no prayers, no sighs; those who fall must raise themselves; the sick must of their own force recover or perish. When thus she has set us upon our legs everything works for us, and the sun and moon are great lamps for our enlightenment, and men and women leaves of a wondrous book. Then, imperceptibly to us, in these snows and blossoms and fruits annually all history is rewritten, and the honest man who knows nothing of Greece and Rome derives from the swelling trees and the bending sky the same subtle infusion of heroism and nobility that is the vitality of history. The vice of our mode of education is that we do not regard life from an eternal point. We want magnanimity and truth, not the names of those who have been magnanimous and true; and I see not why nature to-day does not offer to me all the grandeur of character that has illustrated any period. Men and nature and art all seek to say the same thing. Could we search deeply enough, I doubt not we should find all matter to be one substance; and could we appreciate the worth of every art and every landscape and man, they would be identical. As I am a better man, the more soluble is the great outspreading riddle of nature, and the more distinct and full the delicate grace of art. As an old, quaint divine said of fate and free-will, they are two converging lines which of necessity must somewhere unite, though our human vision does not see the point; so all mysteries are radii, and could we follow one implicitly, then we have found the centre of all. Therefore the best critic of art is the man whose life has been hid with God in nature; and therefore the triumph of art is complete when birds peck at the grapes.

I felt this yesterday while looking at Cole's paintings. Each picture of "The Voyage of Life" impressed me somewhat as the voyage itself does. Especially the cold, subdued tone of the last, which suggests infinity by the tone merely. Perhaps you have not seen them, and will suffer a brief account. The pictures are four. The first represents a boat of golden prow and sides wrought into the images of the hours, bearing an infant in a bed of roses, and issuing from a dim cave in a dark, indefinable mountain, and hasting down a flower-crowned stream. The second shows the babe grown to manhood, and, assuming himself the guidance, leaves the guardian spirit upon the bank, and upon a wider stream, piercing a wider prospect, sails away, allured by a dim cloud-castle which seems to hang over the river, yet from which the stream turns. The next shows him dashing along amid clouds and whirlpools and tempests, without rudder or compass, towards threatening rocks, yet serenely, with clasped hands, abiding the issue. In the last, grown to old age, he sails forth upon a fathomless, shoreless sea, leaving behind all rocks and tempests, while the guardian angel again at the helm points to regions of cloudless day. Though very beautiful of themselves, they suggested to me grander pictures of this grandest theme, and so interested me very much.

Truly there is nothing final; all is suggestive. When, entranced in summer woods, we demand that nature lend our homes somewhat of her beauty, she replies to us that beauty is so subtle, residing not in the green of this leaf nor in the curve of that branch, and not in the whole, but in the soul that contemplates it, that of herself she has none, and that we her lovers have invested her with such golden charms. The universal wish to realize is only typified by the grasping gain. Most men live to acknowledge in heart the superiority of young dreams over old possessions; and the world feels that in the unshrinking aspirations of the youth lies the hope of the world. That is the lightning that purifies the dense atmosphere, and, glancing for an instant, reveals the keenest light known to men. So the old year sings to me as it goes crowned with crystals and snow-drops to its end. Without shrinking, without sorrow, it folds its white garment around unwithered limbs, and submits gracefully to the past. Nature regards it with that calm face whereon no emotions are written, but a wise serenity forever sits. This year, too, is to many lonely hearts a redeemer; and no heavens will be darkly clouded when it is over, but still stars will shine unsurprised.

Pale scholars in midnight vigils, golden gayety wreathing the hours with flowers and gems, unbending sorrow pressing heavy seals upon yielding wretchedness, it will steal surely from all these, and on the morrow be a colorless ghost in the distant past. Its constancy will secure our immortality. The grandeur of the year may be the strength of our character; and as the East receives it, we may enter the inscrutable future reverently and with folded hands.

Sunday. I am going to F. Rakemann's to pass the afternoon and give him this for you. He proposes to pass a week in Boston. I have heard Wallace during the week. He has great talent; but I had heard Ole Bull, and Wallace's violin-playing was only good. What think you of Vieuxtemps, who, I see, is in Boston? Shall you not send Knoop hither? So many things I would say! It is wiser to say nothing. Remember me to my West Roxbury friends, Mrs. Russell and Mrs. Shaw and their spouses.

Ever your friend,

G. W. C.

VIII

N. Y., Thursday, January 18, '44.

I have not yet answered your letter by W. H. Channing in words, though I have said a great deal to you that you have not heard. What an interrupter of conversation is this absence! Neither have I told you of my Vieuxtemps experience, nor shall I close my letter without speaking of Knoop, who by the gods' favor concerts to-night. Your letter by W. H. Channing crystallized a resolution which has been quiet in me for the winter, so still that it needed only a powerful jerk to induce crystallization at once. So the day or two succeeding its receipt found me busy in expressing some thoughts about reform and association which I meant for *The Present*. But the necessity for expression seems to have been satisfied without publication. The essay remains as quietly in my portfolio as did the idea in my mind. So it was with an article on Ole Bull that I wrote some weeks since for the *Tribune*. The need seems to give the thought expression and form, whether it then lay still or fly abroad upon paper wings. Besides, printing does give a dignity to thoughts that the author should feel that they deserve, a permanency too. The newspaper that escapes the turmoil and tear and dust of years bears the same aspect as all its fellows of the same date that were ushered into the morning parlors with it; and so some commentator on Ole Bull and Vieuxtemps or what not shall run down to the lower generations more noiselessly, yet as certainly, as Shakespeare and Plato. There is a

singular pleasure, too, in publishing what nobody thinks is yours. It is addressing the world
not as Geo. Curtis, but as some distinguished
messenger, the mystery of whom is a charm, if
nothing more. Yet unfortunate me! I could
never maintain the secret long. Is that from
pride or because you cannot endure to see men
go wrong, if you can help them? When Charles
Dana came running to me with what he thought
Emerson's poem, how could I help saying, "It
is mine." In that case, at least, it was sympathy for Emerson's reputation that prompted the
speech.

There is something that pleases me much in the
united works of young authors. Sands and who?
in our country published "Yamoyden" and
some other poems together. C. Lamb and Lloyd
(was not Coleridge one?) published some small
verses in company. There is a sort of mean-
ness in it, too, as if they should say, "Here
we come, two scribblers, not worthy singly to
attract your attention, but together making out
something worth your money." After all, a single failure may be better than a double respectability. Imagine the united literary works of
Dwight and Curtis rotting in an odd drawer of
Ticknor's or James Munroe's; could we ever
look each other in the face again? What a still,
perpetual suspicion there would be that the one
swamped the other.

Do you not mean some day to gather your musical essays together, like a whorl of leaves, and suffer them to expand into a book, though not with the cream-colored calyx that Ticknor affects, I beg. Nay, might you not make some arrangements with Greeley to publish them here, in a cheap way, if you would make money, for those who valued them would of course obtain more durable copies. If not, and you would think dignity compromitted, some of the regular publishers might be diplomatized with. They would make an unique work. You know we have nothing similar in American literature, no book of artistic criticism, have we? Why will you not think of it, if you have not done so? And what so poor a man as Hamlet is may do, you shall command. How recreant am I to this noble art, that listen only and celebrate with feeble voice its charms.

Tuesday evening, at a small musical party, I heard Euphrasia Borghese sing, whom you may have heard, and who is to be Prima Donna at the new Opera-house, which opens on the 25th or 26th of the present month. They begin with the "Puritani." It will be altogether devoted to Italian music, I suppose, from the tendency of the New York taste and the collection of musicians.

I heard Vieuxtemps both times he played after his return. I was very much delighted; he was so modest and composed and refined. His playing is as wonderful as Ole Bull's, but not so fascinating; his compositions more contemplative and regular, not so wild and throbbing with the irregular pulsations of unsatisfied genius, as are Ole Bull's. I felt no disposition to compare, feeling how different they were. I thanked God when I came away that no one man has sole power, but that many may serve in this boundless temple, each in its various offices. Yet in my memory is Ole Bull the only man who has stirred me up as genius always must. When I heard Vieuxtemps, I knew what to anticipate; the grandeur of the instrumental and the human possibility upon it had been revealed to me, therefore he could not surprise me, and for that revelation I am indebted to Ole Bull. Vieuxtemps prolonged the echo of the deep tone that had been sounded into my spiritual ear. I must say that the first was grandest to me, and remains so.

I passed Sunday P.M. with Rakemann; he played all the time, told me of you and Boston and his love for it, asked me if I had heard more of the concerts you mentioned. Timm on Monday played me the " Invitation to the W." very beautifully, beside some Mazurkas of Chopin, also the "Egmont" overture grandly. Saturday evening the second Philharmonic, the " Jupiter. Symphony," and some Septuats, etc. It was not a good concert. Castellan sang for the last time. Not a note of Beethoven! Yesterday afternoon and evening I passed with Josephine Maman, who plays and sings finely. We had some of Beethoven, the "Pathetique," etc., and some songs of Schubert, which I had never heard. A singular girl, but delightful to me. My musical appetite has been well appeased; can it ever be satisfied? To-night, Knoop, for whom I have left little space, especially as I find my paper is torn.

Evening. Have just come from Knoop's. It was beautiful to see the worthy mate of such men as Ole Bull and Vieuxtemps. From what you and others had told me, I knew I should like him. So calm and grand. Yet when I left the room a mournful feeling came over me, that so he must leave and be heard no more. Beethoven is not done when he is dead, nor Raphael nor Shakespeare; but for him whose glory is action, which leaves no trace but upon the heart, what shall remain? The notes he may transcribe for others, but the charm of the musical artist lies not therein; it is a personal effluence; how shall we measure it? I felt to-night that he played not for an audience, but to the private heart. He was singing to me his deep searching thought, his star-lost aspiration. Indeed, he is worthy to close the brilliant winter; a calm planet fading from us, but with a mild, steady lustre that condemns sorrow. How invisible, insensibly proceeds his fame! My character must needs be strengthened and mellowed by such men, and so my influence upon others is moulded, till perhaps it meets him again. Surrounded by these intimate relations, we cannot touch one but all thrill. In such a subtle shrine is the influence of genius fitly embalmed and there worshipped. How grand an era in my life, when through a winter I may justly use the word genius many times!

Good-night!

G. W. C.

I am 24! Will you write me the numbers of the "Tempest" sonata, and some others that I liked particularly? The op. 14, No. 2, I have got, and Timm played it to me on Monday. How inexorable is this space, that will not let me crowd in that I am ever your friend,

G. W. C.

IX

N. Y., Sunday evening, Feb. 25, '44.

Do you remember ever to have read a novel called "The Collegians?" A work of great interest, and displaying great dramatic power. I was always anxious to know the author, and chance has thrown his name and history in my way. It was Gerald Griffin, an Irishman of genius, who lived the varied life of a professed literary man. Desirous of having his dramas accepted at the London theatres, and finding no one to favor him. Too noble to be dependent, and going days without food. In 183ty something he published, "Gisippus," a tragedy, famed of the greatest merit. Finally he became weary of his literary life, and entered an Irish convent, where, within two or three years, he died. His father's family in greater part have removed to America, and his elder brother, a physician of note, has recently published his memoirs, the reviews of which I have happened to meet. The reviews say the usual thing of genius, that his writings were full of promise, and that he might have achieved greatly had he lived. Must not this be always a complaint of genius? Its being, not its expression, has the charm which captivates. The dramas are the least part of Shakespeare, and one would give more to have known him than to study them forever. It must seem to us promising, till we have entered into the fulness of its spirit. The necessity of expressing compromises the dignity of being. God is more pleasing to thought as self-contemplation, rather than creation. Expression is degradation to us, not to the genius. That informs everything with its complete Loveliness. But we who must seek in the expression for it, miss its beauty. Critics complain of

Tennyson that he writes no epic, as if all poets must do the same thing. "Comus" is as Miltonic as the "Paradise Lost;" and the little songs of Shakespeare as wide and fresh as the dramas. The diamond is no less wonderful than the world.

Recently my reading has led me into the old English poetry. A friend gave me a card to the Society Library, the largest in the city; and I have found much good browsing in those fields. I have found "Amadis de Gaul" among the rest, and the complete works of Carew, Suckling, Drayton, Drummond, etc. It has led me to wish some more intimate knowledge of English history, to which I must turn. How imperceptibly and surely spread out these meadows where the rare flowers bloom! There is no end to these threads which place themselves in our hand, and which lead every man of the world his different way. So we sail on through the blue spaces, separate as stars.

And you, they tell me, have joined the association. I supposed you were making some move, and thought this might be it. I am glad that you do so so heartily, and more glad that I can say so. After all, the defiance offered us by the varied positions of our friends is what life needs. Each dissimilar act of my friend, while it does not sever him from me, throws me more sternly upon myself. Can we not make our friendship so fine that it shall be only a sympathy of thought, and let the expression differ, and court it to differ? This ray of the sunlight falls upon summer woods, that sinks into the wintry sea, yet are they brothers. The severe loneliness that has sun and moon in its bosom invites us as the vigorous health of the soul. The beautiful isolation of the rose in its own fragrance is self-sufficient.

Charles wrote Burrill a manly letter during the week. The Arcadian beauty of the place is lost to me, and would have been lost, had there been no change. Seen from this city life, you cannot think how fair it seems. So calm a congregation of devoted men and true women performing their perpetual service to the Idea of their lives, and clothed always in white garments. Though you change your ritual, I feel your hope is unchanged; and though it seems to me less beautiful than the one you leave, it is otherwise to you. There was a mild grace about our former life that no system attains. The unity in variety bound us very closely together. I doubt if we shall be again among you, as I had hoped. I cannot, in thought, lose my hold upon the place without pain not to be spoken of. On the whole, I cannot say, even to you, just what I would about it. It will leak out from the pores of my hands before we have done with each other.

I hear no music here now, except Timm and

Rakemann. Charlotte Dana is here; I have
heard her only once. The opera is a wretched
affair. By-the-by, I gave W. H. Channing an
article for *The Present*, very short, upon music
and Ole Bull. If he publishes it, it will not be
new to you, though I do not remember if I have
talked with you about all at which it hints. I
await orders and manuscripts about the French
stories; though you are very busy, all of you,
just now, perhaps too much so for that business.
The rest stands adjourned. Give my love to
friends.   Yrs ever,

G. W. C.

Will you say to C. Dana that I would like to
come for a short visit — at least, before going
elsewhere; and that as soon as possible, say in
a week. Can I come? If not, ask him to say
when.   Yours,

J. BURRILL CURTIS.

Feb'y 27.

X

NEW YORK, *March* 3, 1844.

Your letter was very grateful to me. I had
supposed the silence would be broken by some
music burst of devotion, and that all friends
would be dearer to you the more imperative

the call upon your strength to battle for the Ideal. It half reproved me for the meagre sheet the same day brought to your hand. And yet could we see how all the forces of heaven and earth unite to shape the particle that floats idly by us, we should never see meagreness more.

I do not think (and what a heresy!) that your life has found more than an object, not yet a centre. The new order will systematize your course; but I do not see that it aids your journey. Is it not the deeper insight you constantly gain into music which explains the social economy you adopt, and not the economy the music? One fine symphony or song leads all reforms captive, as the grand old paintings in St. Peter's completely ignore all sects. Association will only interpret music so far as it is a pure art, as poetry and sculpture and painting explain each other. But necessarily Brook Farm, association and all, do not regard it artistically, but charitably. It regenerates the world with them because it does tangible good, not because it refines. We must view all pursuits as arts before we can accomplish.

With respect to association as a means of reform, I have seen no reason to change my view. Though, like the monastic, a life of devotion, to severe criticism it offers a selfish and an unheroic aspect. When your letter first spoke of your personal interest in the movement, I had written you a long statement of my thought, which I did not send, and then partly spun into an article for *The Present*, which I did not entirely finish. It was only a strong statement of Individualism, which would not be new to you, perhaps, and the essential reason of which could not be readily treated. What we call union seems to me only a name for a phase of individual action. I live only for myself; and in proportion to my own growth, so I benefit others. As Fourier seems to me to have postponed his life, in finding out how to live, so I often felt it was with Mr. Ripley. Besides, I feel that our evils are entirely individual, not social. What is society but the shadow of the single men behind it. That there is a slave on my plantation or a servant in my kitchen is no evil; but that the slave and servant should be unwilling to be so, that is the difficulty. The weary and the worn do not ask of me an asylum, but aid. The need of the most oppressed man is strength to endure, not means of escape. The slave toiling in the Southern heats is a nobler aspect of thought than the freed black upon the shore of England. That is just now the point which pains me in association, its lack of heroism. Reform is purification, forming anew, not forming again. Love, like genius, uses the means that are, and the opportunities of to-day. If paints are wanting, it draws charcoal heads with Michael Angelo. These crooked features of society we cannot rend and twist into a Roman outline and grace; but they may be animated with a soul that will utterly shame our carved and painted faces. A noble man purges these present relations, and does not ask beautiful houses and landscapes and appliances to make life beautiful. In Wall Street he gives another significance to trade; in the City Hall he justifies its erection; in the churches he interprets to themselves the weekly assembly of citizens. He uses the pen with which, just now, the coal-man scrawled his bill, and turns off an epic with the fife that in the band so sadly pierced our ears. He moves our trudging lives to the beauties of golden measures. He laughs heartily at our absorbing charities and meetings, upon which we waste our health and grow thin. He answers our distressing plea for the rights of the oppressed, and the "all-men-born-to-be-free-and-equal" with a smiling strength, which assures us therein lies the wealth and the equality which we are trying to manufacture out of such materials as association, organization of society, copartnership, no wages, and the like. While this may be done, why should we retire from the field behind the walls which you offer? Let us die battling or victorious. And this, true for me and you, is true to the uttermost. The love which alone can make

your Phalanx beautiful, also renders it unnecessary. You may insure food and lodgings to
the starving beggar, I do not see that strength
is afforded to the man. Moreover, a stern divine justice ordains that each man stand where
he stands, and do his utmost. Retreat, if you
will, behind this prospect of comfortable living,
but you do so at a sacrifice of strength. Your
food must be eternal, for your life is so. I do
not feel that the weary man outworn by toil
needs a fine house and books and culture and
free air ; he needs to feel that his position, also,
is as good as these. When he has, by a full
recognition of that, earned the right to come to
you, then his faith is deeper than the walls of
association, and the desolate cellar is a cheerful
room for his shining lore. Men do not want opportunities, they do not want to start fair, they
do not want to reach the same goal; they want
only perfect submission. The gospel now to be
preached is not, " Away with me to the land
where the fields are fair and the waters flow,"
but, " Here in your penury, while the rich go
idly by and scoff, and the chariot wheels choke
you with dust, make here your golden age."

> "Who cannot on his own bed sweetly sleep,
> Can on another's hardly rest."

So sings the saintly George Herbert, no new
thought in these days of ours.

JOHN S. DWIGHT

The effect of a residence at the Farm, I imagine, was not greater willingness to serve in the kitchen, and so particularly assert that labor was divine; but discontent that there was such a place as a kitchen. And, however aimless life there seemed to be, it was an aimlessness of the general, not of the individual life. Its beauty faded suddenly if I remembered that it was a society for special ends, though those ends were very noble. In the midst of busy trades and bustling commerce, it was a congregation of calm scholars and poets, cherishing the ideal and the true in each other's hearts, dedicate to a healthy and vigorous life. As an association it needed a stricter system to insure success; and since it had not the means to justify its mild life, it necessarily grew to this. As reformers, you are now certainly more active, and may promise yourselves heaven's reward for that. That impossibility of severance from the world, of which you speak, I liked, though I did not like that there should be such a protest against the world by those who were somewhat subject to it. This was not my first feeling. When I went, it seemed as if all hope had died from the race, as if the return to simplicity and beauty lay through the woods and fields, and was to be a march of men whose very habits and personal appearance should wear a sign of the coming grace. The longer I stayed, the more surely that thought vanished. I had unconsciously been devoted to the circumstance, while I had earnestly denied its value. Gradually I perceived that only as a man grew deeper and broader could he wear the coat and submit to the etiquette and obey the laws which society demands. Now I feel that no new order is demanded, but that the universe is plastic to the pious hand.

Besides, it seems to me that reform becomes atheistic the moment it is organized. For it aims, really, at that which conservatism represents. The merit of the reformer is his sincerity, not his busy effort to emancipate the slaves or to raise the drunkards. And the deeper his sincerity the more deeply grounded seems to him the order he holds to be so corrupt. God always weighs down the Devil. Therefore the church is not a collection of puzzling priests and deceived people, but the representative, now as much as ever, of the religious sentiment. A pious man needs no new church or ritual. The Catholic is not too formal nor the Quaker too plain. If he complains of these, and build another temple and construct a new service, it is not the satisfaction which piety would have. Luther's protest was that of the intellect against the supremacy of sentiment. So was Unitarianism; and now we do not seek in the Boston churches for the profound pietists. Does not our present experience show that as fast as we

are emancipated from morality and the domi-
nance of the intellect, we revert to the older
rituals, if we need any. And if we have no need,
the piety can so fully inform them, that we seek
no other. The transcendental is a spiritual
movement. It is the effort to regain the lost
equilibrium between the intellect and the soul,
between morals and piety. Therefore, out of its
ranks come Catholics and Calvinists and mystics,
and those who continue the reform movement
commenced by Luther; and, proceeding at intervals down the stream of history, are the Ra-
tionalists. There is indeed a latent movement,
badly represented by these reforms, and that is
the constant perception of the supremacy of the
Individual. But the stronger the feet become
the more delicate may be the movements. The
more strictly individual I am, the more certainly
I am bound to all others. I can reach other
men only through myself. So far as you have
need of association you are injured by it.

You will gather what I think from such
hints as these. I recognize the worth of the
movement, as I do of all sincere action. Other
reasons must bind me peculiarly to the particular me at Brook Farm. "Think not of any severance of our loves," though we should not meet
immediately. Burrill will see if there is any
such place as we wish about you. I have not
much hope of his success. The scent of the

roses will not depart, though the many are scattered. I hardly hope to say directly how very beautiful it lies in my memory. What a heart-fresco it has become! All the dignity, the strength, the devotion will be preserved by you; that graceful "aimlessness" comes no more. And yet that was necessary. Long before I knew of the changes I perceived that the growth of the place would overshadow the spots where the sunlight had lain so softly and long. We must still regret the waywardness of the child, though the man is active and victorious; and the delicate odor of the blossom is unrivalled by the juicy taste of the fruit. The one implies necessity; the other a self-obedient impulse. You see I do not forget it was a child; but the philosopher has no better playfellow.

I wish this was me instead of my letter, for a warm grasp of the hand might say more than all these words.   Yr friend,

G. W. C.

XI

New York, March 27, 1844.

At last I imagine our summer destiny is fixed. This morning Burrill received a reply from Emerson informing us of a promising place near Concord. The farmer's name being Cap-

160

tain Nathaniel Barrett, of pleasant family and situation, and a farm on which more farm work than usual is done. Altogether the prospect is very alluring and satisfactory; and I have little doubt of our acceptance of the situation. We shall not then be very far removed from you; and at some Æsthetical tea or Transcendental club or Poet's assembly meet you, perhaps, and other Brook Farmers. At all events, we shall breathe pretty much the same atmosphere as before, and understand more fully the complete pivacy of the country life.

Burrill brought pleasant accounts of your appearance at Brook Farm. The summer shall not pass without my looking in upon you, though only for an hour. That time will suffice to show me the unaltered beauty of aspect, though days would be scarce to express all that they suggested.

Emerson writes that there is a piano and music at the farm mentioned. I have no faith in pianos under such circumstances; but it shows a taste, a hope, a capability, possibly it is equal to all spiritual significances except music! which want in a piano may be termed a deficiency.

I have become acquainted with a fine amateur, a niece of Dr. Channing's, name Gibbs. She is yet young, not more than 17, but plays with great grace and beauty. She played me

one of Mendelssohn's songs, translated by Liszt,
a beautiful piece, one of F. R.'s, and spoke more
sensibly of music than any girl I have met.   By-
the-way, yesterday I bought the January number of the *Democratic Review* to read Mrs. Fanny Kemble Butler's review of Tennyson, when,
to my great surprise, I found your "Haydn."
O'Sullivan I have met a great deal, but made no
acquaintance.   The Tennyson review is very
fine.   I think she understands him well.   Perhaps she is too masculine a woman to judge
correctly his delicacy; but she does the whole
thing well.

Cranch has just painted a scene from the
"Lady of Shalott," the scene—

> "In among the bearded barley,
>   The reaping late and early," etc.—

represents two reapers standing with sickles
among the grain, and turning intently towards
the four "gray walls and four gray towers which
overlook a space of flowers" in an island covered
with foliage to the water, and lying in the midst
of the stream.   The criticism upon the picture is
obvious; if Cranch is as painter what Tennyson
is as poet, it is good—if not, it is bad.   What do
you think?   When a man illustrates a poem he
is pledged by the poem, hence the absurdity of
Martyn's drawings from the "Paradise Lost,"
and the various pictures of Belshazzar's feast.

Only the Madonnas of the greatest painters are satisfactory. But I shall not abandon myself to the tracking of these mysteries of art.

I have been reading Goethe's "Tasso." Now I am at the "Sorrows of Werther." I am wonderfully impressed with his dramatic power. The "Egmont," "Iphigenia," and "Tasso" are grander than anything I know in modern literature, than anything else of his which I have read. The serene simplicity of the "Iphigenia" is like a keen blast of ocean air. It stands like a Grecian temple, but in the moonlight. Is not that because, as Fanny Kemble says, and so many have thought, he was a Heathen? He did not enter into the state called the Christian. He served gods, not a God; and had it been otherwise this tragedy had been full-bathed in sunlight. And yet I hardly dare to say anything decidedly of such a man. I shall condemn myself a little while hence if I do.

Let me hear from you before I leave New York, which will be in two or three weeks. I shall not leave all my good friends, and all the fine music here, without a pang. But if we stop for pangs! Will you send me the number of the "Mondschein," and the "Tempest" sonata?

Yr friend,

G. W. CURTIS.

XII

N. Y., *Monday morning, April 8th*, 1844.

The last few days have been like glimpses of Brook Farm, seeing so constantly Mr. Ripley, and Charles, and Liszt, and Isaac, and Georgiana, and Margaret Fuller. The last three days of the past week were occupied by the sessions of the Convention, about which there was no enthusiasm, but an air of quiet resolution which always precedes success. To be sure, the success, to me, is the constant hope in humanity that inspires them, the sure, glowing prophecies of paradise and heaven, being individual not general prophecies, and announcing the advent in their own hearts and lives of the feet beautiful of old upon the mountains. In comparison with this what was done, and what was doing, lost much of its greatness. Leave to Albert Brisbane, and *id omne genus,* these practical etchings and phalansteries; but let us serve the gods without bell or candle. Have these men, with all their faith and love, not yet full confidence in love? Is that not strong enough to sway all institutions that are, and cause to overflow with life? does that ask houses and lands to express its power? does it not ride supreme over the abounding selfishness of the world, and so raise men from their

sorrow and degradation, or so inspire them that
their hovels are good enough for them?

But all difference of thought vanished before
the profound, sincere eloquence of these men.
Last night, at W. H. Channing's church, the
room was full, and the risen Lord Jesus might
have smiled upon a worthy worship. From all
sections were gathered in that small room men
led by the same high thought, and in the light of
that thought joining hearts and hands, unknown
to each other, never to be seen again, and in the
early dawn setting forth with hard hands and
stout hearts to hew down the trees which shall
be wrought into the stately dwellings for those
who come after in the day. So knelt the devoted Pilgrims upon the sands of Holland, and
embarked upon that doubtful sea. They fought
and perished; their homes were pierced with the
Indian's bullet and flames of fire; the solitude of
stern forests scared not their hearts, and we follow now and live in peace. It was something to
have felt and seen such heroism.

The meetings of the convention were made
interesting by some speeches of W. H. Channing.
His fervor kindles the sympathy of all who listen.
I do not think he is a man of great intellect; his
views of society are not always correct. He
speaks very often as an infidel-in-the-capability-
of-men might speak. He is fanatical, as all who
perceive by the heart and not the head are, as

deeply pious men are apt to be. But I never heard so eloquent a man, one who commanded attention and sympathy, not by his words or thoughts, but the religion that lay far below them. It is a warm, fragrant, southern wind at which the heart leaps, not the pure, cold, ocean air which braces the frame. Between him and some whom I have heard is the same difference as between Goethe and Novalis. The one a June meadow, with flower-scents and cloud-shadows and the soft, sultry music of humming-bees and singing-birds, with clear skies bending over; a deep sea the other, whereon sail stately ships, wafted by health-bearing breezes, in whose waters the sick gain strength, in whose soundless depths the coral and the precious stones repose forever, which supplies the clouds whose shadow makes the meadow beautiful.

Indeed, how glorious is the range and variety of character among which we move. Though the stars differ in glory they all make the sky fair, and do not clash in their revolutions. That dissimilarity is the secret of friendship, which educates to stand alone. Indeed—to make a most heretical conclusion—the race exists to teach me to live without it. My friend, God has no need of creatures, but he is not less nearly bound to them.

I send you the final number of *The Present*. You will see my article, "a poor thing, but mine own." To you it will be nothing new. It seems to me I have used some of the same sentences in speaking to you.

The Dial stops. Is it not like the going out of a star? Its place was so unique in our literature! All who wrote and sang for it were clothed in white garments; and the work itself so calm and collected, though springing from the same undismayed hope which fathers all our best reforms. But the intellectual worth of the time will be told in other ways, though *The Dial* no longer reports the progress of the day.

On Friday we leave for Boston. I do not know precisely if we shall go immediately to Concord, for we are performing at the same time a duty of affection in accompanying to Mount Auburn the body of an uncle. We may possibly be detained in Boston until the following Monday, in which case I shall not fail to come out and see you.

So endeth my New York correspondence.

Yours truly and ever,

G. W. CURTIS.

MUSIC AND OLE BULL

We know little of the art of music; though our concerts are crowded, and the names of the composers familiar. But our reverence to the

Masters in art is like the reverence for the Bible, not a hearty one. A late musical reviewer well says, that the admiration of the Parisians for Beethoven is a conceit. That calculation answers for our meridian. Slight Italian scholars are eloquent in their admiration of Dante, but the depths and majesty of his poem are explored by few. The dullest may recognize the beauty of feature, but the soul which inspires quite eludes them. During the performance of a symphony the audience smile and shake when the airs float out of the orchestra, not observing that they are the breathing-places, the relaxation of the composer. Every one who can play can compose tunes, but to the lover of the art they yield no greater pleasure than the rhymes of a poem. Often the grandest passages are most melodious, as in poems the greatest thought suggests the happiest expression. Tune and song occupy a distinct portion of the realm of music. They are *attachés* to the royal court. Perhaps the finest music is allied to verse, but if it be a true marriage, the music comprehends the whole. No artist would hear the words of one of Handel's or Haydn's choral hosannas. The words are the translation, but the scholar will not accept that.

Music is an art distinct and self-sufficient. It represents the harmony of that interior truth which all art seeks to reveal, and whose beauty and grace appear in painting and sculpture. The interpreters of that harmony are sounds, which are related to music as colors to painting, and the fullest expression is given to them by instrumental combination. The human voice in respect of the art is valuable as an instrument, and in suppleness may exceed mechanical contrivances; wherefore one readily understands why a mighty chorus is introduced in the finale of the grandest symphony, that the whole effect may be duly crowned, and the appeal to the heart be assured by the union of human sounds. But with such an effect words have nothing to do. The charm of the foreign opera to us Americans is, that the full music of the Masters is received with syllables meaning to us no more than the fa-sol-la of the gamut. The reason of this is very evident. If the poetry be good it has a rhythm and cadence of its own which resembles music, but in respect of art belongs to poetry and not to music. Arbitrarily united with melody the words obtrude a meaning which the music may not suggest, though the capacity of fine music is equal to any words. The beauty of Schubert's songs is their completeness. They are lyrics, and the words are only an addition. Those who heard Rakemann play the translated serenade will remember that the instrumentation produced the whole effect of the song. If the music be fine, it gives all the sentiment of the words in its own way. It is like painting a statue to unite them. Sometimes, indeed, one feels that both are written from the same mood in the grandest minds. The mysterious charms of Goethe's song of Mignon, to which Beethoven wrote the music, is that the song is the expression of the same awe-struck yearning which wails and thunders through the music of the master. In the melody alone all the wild vagueness and dim aspiration of the song are manifest, and only because the union is perfect is the impression uniform. Should Wilhelm Meister be lost to literature the blossom of Mignon's life would still bloom in the music.

The same necessity which divided art into the arts ordains their practical separation. Because they are divisions of one their impression is similar. They work to the same end, but each has a way. To complete the harmony, the soprano, and the tenor, and the bass, must all strictly observe their parts. So must the arts. It is a mournful degradation when the composer would make his sounds, colors, as those who heard the battle of Waterloo symphony will not soon forget. Without his interference, the relation between his art and the rest will be preserved. In his symphony he is the spiritual significance of the Apollo and the Iliad; and the graceful, romantic songs of Mozart are in the drops of poetry scattered upon the old drama, and in the infinite, tender beauty of Raphael's pictures. Yet this is a likeness as between woods and waters, and with which we have nothing to do.

If a reply be sought to the question, why the grandest compositions of this art are more generally impressive than the efforts of the pure science, it may be reached in various ways. The old masters, doubtless, obeyed an unconscious instinct in joining words to their music. Then, as now, the art was in its young years, and the words served as a dictionary to the student. Merely as a dictionary, for the deep significance of the thing could not be apprehended until that was thrown aside, and the scholar read and spoke and lived in that high language as in his daily speech. The best American critic of the art says, speaking of the Messiah, "Feeling that it was time now to do something more worthy his genius, and more fitting his years, as he was getting old, he resolved to draw from all the sources of his art, and put forth all his power, to make an eloquent exposition of his faith in music, and interpret the Bible thus to the hearts of all men." And yet, hitherto, have not the sublime fragments he culled from the Bible served as expositors of the Oratorio? The Messiah is the celebration, in Handel's way, of the great things of his life, which, more or less, are the remarkable experience of all men, and which receive the grandest verbal expression in the Bible. Having this same confession to make, and obeying a different means from Moses and the apostles, a means which few could understand, what remained but to transcribe the sublimest verbal record men knew, and tell them that that was a free translation of his thought. So, in later times, Beethoven replied to one who asked the meaning of a sonata, "Read Shakespeare's Tempest." With the masses and operas of modern times the case is the same. Genius, which is plenitude of power, adapts itself to all facts. It will receive the outline of a story and weave upon it a wonderful web, which the story shall interpret. But an opera of Mozart's reveals to the voiceless player its whole magnificence. Trilling Prima Donnas and silvery Italian are the addenda and vocabulary. They are the "this is the man, this the beast" written under the picture. The severe beauty of the art is immediately injured by any encroachment upon the others. The highest praise awarded to the most successful of such attempts is that of imitation. Haydn would represent the growing of grass and the budding of trees — a beautiful conceit, but a false perception of his art. Art has little to do with imitation. The best portrait is not the fac-simile of a face, but the suggestion of a character. Music has not to do with form but thought. The Germans derive no more pleasure from the songs of their masters than we who may not know their language.

The second question is that of persons who do not understand the claims of music to the dignity of an art, whom pleasant old songs pleasantly lull to sleep after dinner; to whom comes no voice of the art separate from all things else, but which stands before him silent and veiled, while an interpreter converses. Often these songs are beautiful ballads, and so have a peculiar grace. If the music is appropriate and simple and melodious it is enough, and henceforth, to such, no artist who does not play tunes is more than a quack; and the complaint of the man who sat hearing Ole Bull for an hour, and then departed because he was so long tuning his fiddle, is the most general criticism upon his performance. But the old Scotch and Irish airs, which endear these songs to us, were doubtless, at some remote period, the wordless singings of maternal love over the rocking-cradle. They become readily united with words as a help to the memory, and as imparting facility of expression. Those who have heard "Auld Robin Gray," "Robin Adair," and the airs which Moore has gratefully accompanied with words, played on summer evenings, with flutes and horns, then realize that the impression lies in that which the words shadow. This fact is recognized in modern music by the introduction of songs without words — by the composition and performance, with more or less success, of Beethoven's symphonies, where most of all words are at fault. The pleasure of him to whom these profound compositions reveal a meaning is more private and enchanting than any he knows. He is very well content to be called enthusiastic, for his presence along justifies the performance of such works. When he meets at the concert-room those who are enraptured with Donizetti, yet who come to do homage to Beethoven, he is reminded that Beethoven would not see Rossini, holding him as one who debased the art; and it seems to him like Jesus calling upon the Jews to become as little children. Everybody reads Shakespeare, but few know what the word means. The theatre is crowded to hear Macready's "Hamlet," but it is to see Macready, not to study the drama. When he is gone the play remains; and though it is spoken by stupid men, their dulness cannot affect its profundity and strength. That is the test of art, that it transcends its instruments; and the artist at his piano realizes the soul, though not the effect of the symphony which has spoken to him so loudly from the orchestra.

The music written at this day is gymnastics for the instrument, rather than worthy offerings upon the altar of art. It is a perverse separation of the art and the science. It requires an accurate knowledge of the instrument that it may surprise, and so win applause for the performer; not that it may the better serve music, whether it has auditors or not. Few things could have more deeply pained a worthy musician than the last concert of Max Böhrer. Such profound knowledge of the power of the instrument, such utter ignorance of its intention. It seemed to groan in despair, that he, who knew its changes so well, could not awaken it to melody, but, with solemn conceit, show that he did know them, and gain approbation for that knowledge. Knoop, with the same exact science, showed a hearty reverence for art, and reverently withdrew himself and his violoncello. Castellan's voice was so full that her person was necessarily forgotten. One would not do injustice to the voice; that is frequently the instrument for which fine music is written; but in view of the art, it is an instrument only. Its deeper effect upon many minds springs from its humanity, from that part of it of which nothing can be said, and which the coal-man has as well as Malibran. This constitutes its occasional superiority of influence, but cannot impart to it the effect and artistic manifestation which instruments produce. When the full force of both is united, as in the symphony mentioned, the grandest musical expression appears.

The winter has been full of finer musical

experience than we have yet had. With Ole Bull, Vieuxtemps, and Knoop, Castellan and Damoreau—the Beethoven symphonies and German overtures of the Philharmonic Society, the art has reached a point hitherto unattained. Yet this is partly deceptive. Most persons heard Ole Bull from curiosity, and the symphonies from fashion. Such music and such artists have no permanent hold of the heart here. The pianos are covered with the songs of Donizetti; and Max Böhrer takes, generally, a higher rank than Knoop. The student of art does not regard these noble artists and fine music as the dawning of the art among us, but as brighter stars flashing across the sky, while still the east is dark. Europe has made these artists and this music after many centuries. In the bosom of a church, full of profound spiritual experiences, this music has been nurtured, and artistic devotion has streamed upon these men. The necessity of this hoary antiquity to the development of art we cannot readily determine. Our painters and sculptors must flock to Italy, and lie down in the shadows of those old fanes, before they are willing to announce their claim to be servants of the art. Our poets sing in self-defence the majesty and grandeur of primeval America, and drink deeply at the stream of letters that flows from the Past. Had foreign literature been cut off from us, we should have

JOHN S. DWIGHT

had few writers of poetry, and Mr. Griswold's
book had been a valuable duodecimo and not a
heavy octavo. Our chief poets are cultivated
men. Poetry with us is the recreation of elegant scholars. Mr. Percival announces that he
writes poetry in more than a hundred ways; and
the few young men who seem to advance first
claims to the dignity of poets, by their fresh expression, need the overshadowing of Time to
make them artists. How especially is this so
with music. We have no native artists and few
hearty students. The societies which introduce
to us the finest music are German, our musical
teachers are Germans and Italians, our opera is
Italian. Of this no complaint is to be made.
The nation is content with a foreign fragrance,
as the individual students are content to live in
Rome and send home to us the ideas of an old
mythology wrought into statues. Art is the
flower of life. The man will build his house,
then he will have pictures and a piano. The
claims of the interior life will surely be heard at
last, and art will follow. Yankees and Wall
Street govern now, Niagara by-and-by. The
prophecies of our American literature, with
which the literary anniversaries are annually eloquent, are sure. Contemplating the healthy
seed which they represent, we need not fear for
the flower. But the literature and art will be
American only in respect of culture. The Ger-

M   177

man music is an universal song, sung in a provincial dialect. The immortality of the classics is the universality of their truth. English and Italian art are the several ways that nations regard the same thing. The soul of music, as of painting and poetry, is always one. The foreigner is no longer a foreigner when he hears the music he loves; and silent under its spell, lovers, for the first time, meet. In the Louvre or the Vatican will not the traveller see his home?

Yet in our present backwoods life let me not omit to notice the wonderful artist whom we have recently seen. The genius of Ole Bull is so delicate and profound that we must speak of it modestly, but with certainty. It is not to be estimated by comparison. The height assures us of its loftiness, not by the inferior summits below it, but by the wide, full sunlight and the free winds that flow around it and rest upon it. The perception of genius is so sure that we need not attempt to define what it is. Every artist, full of its power, shows something more than the last. Like beauty, it will not be measured, but every beautiful person shames our analysis and philosophy of beauty. Yet the impression of genius is always the same, and its appearance in any one individual makes real to us all the rest. Until we heard Ole Bull, Paganini was a fabulous being of whom, as of Or-

pheus and Amphion, strange stories were told,
which seemed rather prophecies of musical possibility than the history of actual accomplishment. Henceforth Paganini is a household god,
and the old Pagans loom more distinctly through
the misty centuries and wear something of the
aspect of reality.

To us, children of a seventy years' nation,
plucking the full blossom of European musical
culture, the appearance of Ole Bull was like a
new star in the sky. Few had predicted its shining. At most, there was a faint hope, in some
minds, that we should yet see a worthy minister
of art, in honoring whom we should fitly reverence the Masters. Yet it was a hope too faint
and limited to inspire confidence in our manager
to secure to himself a fair portion of the ample
harvest nodding for so sharp a sickle. When he
appeared, that wild Norwegian bravery, subdued
by a reverence for art and deepened by commanding originality, the shouting theatre, the
crowded tabernacle, the press for once speaking
confidently in one tone, the silent joy of hearts
to whom this was the first vision of genius—these
announced a triumph. The ecstatic musical
festivals of Europe, the pilgrimages of artists
more royally surrounded than the progress of
kings, we now understood.

The chief value of Ole Bull is that he introduces us more nearly to art. It is the preroga-

tive of genius to illustrate that; therefore he stood before us as one who had in rapt hours pierced a little further into the mystery which envelops life like an atmosphere and came to recite his vision. He had detected some of those fine sunbeams that make the air golden and give it warmth, and painted them for us as well as he could. Yet in his music there was the same melancholy strain, varied by wonderful and wild freaks, like the hysterics of the gods, that hitherto so emphatically characterizes the works of genius. Throughout his compositions there was the want of unity which expressed aspiration not fulfil-ment, scattered stones of a fairer temple than men have seen, which also are all works of art hitherto, yet each so fair that for these the old shrines are deserted, and here men worship. One perceived that the performance was the least part of the man. It was not his height and limit, a faint beacon-light, rather, trembling over the waters, marking the shore of a wide land, with deep ravines and towering mountains and endless woods fringing depthless seas, and yet a light so bright that we thought the sun was rising. For the genius which enables one to il-lustrate art is universal power, whose expression is inadequate because thought is quicker than execution. Every work of art represents an era past. Only the whole character of the artist is the present flower of his life. It is no matter of surprise that Ole Bull practises little, that his compositions are unique. A deep rhythm, a subdued, infinite harmony pervades them. The rugged Norway shows in them its influence upon the artist. The rocks and glens and forests of his fatherland are not painted, but their spiritual significance floats through his music, modified and moulded by the individuality of the man. All this appears in his aspect. As he advances, the strong, composed grace of his appearance, deferential not to individuals but to the mind which shall receive the song of his inspiration, destroys conventional ideas of grace, as Mont Blanc might destroy them. His tall, compact figure well becomes a priest of art. Out of his eyes shines the reflection of the perpetual fire of which all artists are the ministers and which communicates energy and warmth to his action. With a slight, respectful motion of the head and violin-bow towards the orchestra, the respect of Olympian power, he draws from them the first notes of the symphony; then, leaning his head upon his instrument caressingly, as if he gratefully heard at once what he is about to unfold to the audience, he draws his bow. Then that violin expresses with intense passion the undefined yearnings that haunt the private heart. It entreats and restrains. Its wildness harmonizes with the deep unrest of a great aspiring soul. Its solemn movement is like the progress of a brave man to an unknown destiny, and as the last yet distinct cadence floats away into the stillness, it is as if a dove disappeared in heaven. At his second concert he played an adagio of Mozart. It was full of tender delicacy and the graceful imagination that makes all his music romance. All this the artist felt, and every tone that followed his bow was exquisite. Then was it seen how all genius meets. It was as if the composer lay in the violin and sang the song anew, as if Raphael recited one of Shakespeare's sonnets.

With what has been said about the man one who realizes the genius has little to do. The music was not false, and that is his language. There has been stern opposition and prejudice and ill-will; but so we must all bring our gifts to the altar, and they who have not gold gifts must tender swine.

Not the least of his offices is that he has enabled us to appreciate Vieuxtemps. They will not be compared by the reverent worshipper at the shrine of art. The plant needs the sunshine and the dew. It was pleasant to feel that genius abides in one man and realize that one star differeth from another in glory. Surely the firmament of art is wide enough and yet deep enough to contain many planets.

Yet the artists are but messengers whom we send before into the undiscovered country. They return and sing to us songs familiar in the Eldo-

rado of our hope, yet of which we have learned
no note. Afloat upon the depthless sea we loose
doves and ravens, who bear back to us olive
boughs and flowers which we cannot analyze,
but whose form and fragrance make our homes
beautiful. When the first shock of delighted
wonder is past we receive great men as the present attainment of an illimitable Nature, as the
Earth receives the light of stars, unnoticed save
of wandering lovers, and sweeps undisturbed on
its way. If sometimes we are warped from our
sphere by the apparition of noble persons, wise
men presently recover themselves and serve with
a milder and firmer persistence their own nature.
The way is made clearer by these bright lights,
universal nature is fairer that there are so many
single stars; but they must be only stars in our
heaven and fires on our hearth, nor turn out the
heart by inserting themselves in the bosom.

G. W. C.

XIII

CONCORD, *Friday evening*, *May 10th*, 1844.

Since our arrival here I have been busy
enough. From breakfast at 6 to dinner at $12\frac{1}{2}$,
hard at work, and all the afternoon roaming over
the country far and near. When we came the
spring was just waking, now it is opening like a

rose-bud, with continually deepening beauty. The apple-trees in full bloom, making the landscape so white, seem to present a synopsis of the future summer glory of the flower-world.

Our farm lies on one of the three hills of Concord. They call it Punkatassett. Before us, at the foot of the hill, is the river; and the slope between holds a large part of the Captain's orchard. Among the hills at one side we see the town, about a mile away; and a wide horizon all around, which Elizabeth Hoar tells me she has learned is the charm of Concord scenery. The summit of the hill on which we are is crowned with woods, and from a clearing commands a grand prospect. Wachusett rises alone upon the distance, and takes the place of the ocean in the landscape. There is a limitation in the prospect if one cannot see the sea or mountains. The Blue Hill, in a measure, supplies that want at West Roxbury. Otherwise the landscape is a garden which only pleases. We are much pleased with our host and his family. He is that Capt. Nathan Barrett to whom Messrs. Pratt and Brown came for seed, and who raises a good deal of seed for Ruggles, Nourse and Mason. We go into all work. The Captain turns us out with the oxen and plough, and we do our best. Already I have learned a good deal. The men are very courteous and generous.

Indeed, I am disposed to think it just the place

we wanted. As yet I see no reason to doubt it.
It is so still a life after the city, and after the
family at Brook Farm. I am glad to be thrown
so directly and almost alone into nature, and am
more ready than ever to pay my debt in a human way by learning the names of her beautiful
flowers and the places where they blossom. We
study Botany daily, and have thus far kept pace
with the season. I have found here the yellow
violet, which I do not remember at West Roxbury. Already we have the rhodora and the col-
umbine, which you have probably found. And
with our afternoons surrendered to the meadows
and hills, and our mornings to the fields, we find
no heavy hours; but every Sunday surprises us. I
am to bed at 9, and rise at $4\frac{1}{2}$ or 5. I practise the
Orphic, which says: "Baptize thyself in pure wa-
ter every morning when thou leavest thy couch,"
which I more concisely render, Wash betimes.

For the last three evenings I have been in
the village, hearing Belinda Randall play and
sing. With the smallest voice she sings so delicately, and understands her power so well, that I
have been charmed. It was a beautiful crown to
my day, not regal and majestic, like Frances O.'s
in the ripe summer, but woven of spring flowers
and buds. Last night I saw her at Mr. Hoar's,
only herself and Miss E. Hoar, G. P. Bradford,
Mr. and Mrs. Emerson, and myself and Mr.
Hoar. She played Beethoven, sang the "Ade-

laide Serenade," "Fischer Madchen," "Amid this Green Wood." I walked home under the low, heavy, gray clouds; but the echo lingered about me like starlight.

We have a piano in the house, and a very good one. It was made by Currier, and is but a few years old. The evenings do not all pass without reminding me of the flute music of the last summer, and making me half long to hear it again. Yet I am too contented to wish to be back at the Farm. The country about us is wilder than there; but I need now this tender severity of nature and of friendship. With John Hosmer, Isaac, Geo. Bradford, and Burrill, I am not without some actual features of the Farm as I knew it. When I shall see you I cannot say. I shall not willingly break the circle of life here, though occasion will make me willing enough.

Let me not remain unmentioned to my friends at Brook Farm and in the village; and when you can *ungroup* yourself for an hour paint me a portrait of the life you lead.

Yr friend,

G. W. C.

XIV

CONCORD, *May 24th,* '44.

MY DEAR FRIEND,—I heard of you at Ole Bull's concert, and have sympathized with you in your delight. I was in Worcester that evening, and had hoped to have come down to Boston and heard him once more. But so many were listening with that pleasure which can come but once, and I knew so many must try in vain to hear, that I was content others should then express that admiration which lies so deeply in my heart. But who of all heard? Was it not as if he walked above the earth, and of his sublime conversation you heard now and then the notes? Did not the singular beauty of the man unite with his performance to make the completest musical festival you have had?

Indeed, I owe more to him than one can know, except as he feels the same debt; are you not that one?

To Belinda Randall, who has been here, as I told you, I was obliged for revealing Beethoven's tenderness. She is so soft and tender herself that she could not fail unconsciously to express it in her playing. I passed some fine evenings with her. Since I had been here I had heard no music, and felt that I needed to hear some as an adequate expression of all that I felt. When she came that demand was satisfied. Ole Bull satisfies the claim of the same nature which our whole life makes, and of itself creates, rather reveals newer and deeper demands, and so on, I suppose, until the celestial harmonies are heard by us.

I heard from a friend of the last Philharmonic

in New York. It seems they have made Vieux-temps an honorary member, and he played for them. On the same evening they performed one of Beethoven's symphonies. It is one of those accounts whose beauty is their nakedness. To lovers of music a bare description is as an outline to a painter which he can readily fill up and supply with the shadows and sunlight. Yet not he so magnificently as sunlight and shadows sweep over this landscape. It seems to me that a century of splendor has been rushing by since I have been here.

The persons who make Concord famous I have hardly seen. The consciousness of their presence is like the feeling of lofty mountains whom the night and thick forests hide. Of one of them, E. Hoar, I need to say nothing to you. One evening I sat with her and Waldo Emerson and Geo. P. Bradford while Belinda Randall played and sang.

Isaac brings you this, and will himself best tell you of himself. Burrill is well, and unites with me in remembrance to all who remember.

Your friend,

G. W. C.

XV

CONCORD, *June 26th*, 1844.

These are Tophetic times. I doubt if the sturdy faith of those heroes, Shadrack and co.,

JOHN S. DWIGHT

would carry them through this fervor unliquefied. Their much vaunted furnace was but a cool retreat where thoughts of great-coats were possible, compared with this. And if that nether region of whose fires so much is sung by poets and other men possessed, can offer hotter heats, let them be produced. Those Purgatorial ardencies for the gentle suggestion of torment to thin shades can have little in common with these perspiration-compelling torridities. Why does not some ingenious Yankee improve such times for the purchase, at a ruinous discount, of all thick clothes? I tremble lest some one should offer me an ice-cream for my best woollens! Is it human to resist such an offer? Does it not savor something of Devildom, and a too great familiarity with that lower Torrid Zone, to entertain such a proposition cool-ly? when such a word grows suddenly obsolete in such seasons? If I venture to move, such an atmosphere of heat is created immediately around my body that all cool breezes (if the imagination is competent to such a conception) are like arid airs when they reach my mouth. Perhaps we are tending to those final, fiery days of which Miller is a prophet. We are slowly sinking, perhaps, from heat to heat, until entire rarefication and evanishment in imperceptible vapor ensues; and so the great experiment of a world may end in smoke, as many minor ones have ended. If it were not so hot, I should love to think about these things.

June 28th. So far I had proceeded on the afternoon I returned to Concord. When I desisted I supposed I had inscribed my final manuscript, and that only a cinder would be found sitting over it when some one should enter. Yet by the providence of God I am preserved for the experience of greater heats. I did not know before what was the capacity of endurance of the human frame. I begin to suspect we are of nearer kin to the Salamander than our pride will allow; and since Devils only are admitted to nether fire, I begin to lapse into the credence of total depravity!! Reflect upon my deplorable condition! As Shelley's body, when lifeless, was caused to disappear in flames and smoke, so may mine before its tenant is departed. Was it not prophetic that on Sunday afternoon the following lines came to me while thinking of that poet?

SHELLEY

A smoke that delicately curled to heaven,
　Mingling its blueness with the infinite blue,
So to the air the faded form was given,
　So unto fame the gentle spirit grew.

And as Shelley and Keats are associated always together in my mind, immediately the Muse gave me this:

JOHN S. DWIGHT

KEATS

A youth did plight his troth to Poesy.
 "Thee only," were the fervent words he said,
Then sadly sailed across the foaming sea,
 And lay beneath the southern sunset dead.

I was glad that once I could express what I think about those men. These will show you, but you must write your own poem upon them before you will be satisfied. Is it not so always? We cannot speak much about poets until our thought of them sings itself.

The day I left you was very hot in Boston. Anna Shaw and Rose Russell passed me like beautiful spirits; one like a fresh morning, the other like an Oriental night. Then I did my business, and met James Sturgis, who carried me to see his head cut in cameo by Mr. King. It is quite good, though it gives him rather a finer head than he has; but that's a good failing. I went to the Athenæum. There I saw one or two pictures, and much paint upon canvas. Those that I liked I saw belonged to the Athenæum, and I suppose were old objects to those who are familiar with the gallery. A face of Ophelia interested me. It was very simple and sweet. But I was so warm that I could do little more than lay upon a bench and catch dreamy glimpses of the walls. The sculpture gallery, full of white marble heads, seemed quite cool.

My dear friend, I shall melt and be mailed in
this letter as a spot if I do not surcease. May
you be blest with frigidity, a blessing far removed from my hope. Of course I must be
warmly, nay, *hotly* remembered to Charles.

Yrs ever,

G. W. C.

XVI

CONCORD, August 7th, 1844.

My regret at not seeing you was only les-
sened by the beautiful day I passed with Mr.
Hawthorne. His life is so harmonious with the
antique repose of his house, and so redeemed
into the present by his infant, that it is much
better to sit an hour with him than hear the
Rev. Barzillai Frost! His baby is the most serenely happy I ever saw. It is very beautiful,
and lies amid such placid influences that it too
may have a milk-white lamb as emblem; and
Mrs. Hawthorne is so tenderly respectful towards her husband that all the romance we picture
in a cottage of lovers dwells subdued and dignified with them. I see them very seldom. The
people here who are worth knowing, I find, live
very quietly and retired. In the country, friendship seems not to be of that consuming, absorbing character that city circumstances give it, but

to be quite content to feel rather than hear or do; and that very independence which withdraws them into the privacy of their homes is the charm which draws thither.

Mr. Emerson read an address before the anti-slavery "friends" last Thursday. It was very fine. Not of that cold, clear, intellectual character which so many dislike, but ardent and strong. His recent reading of the history of the cause has given him new light and warmed a fine enthusiasm. It commenced with allusions to the day "which gives the immense fortification of a fact to a great principle," and then drew in strong, bold outline the progress of British emancipation. Thence to slavery in its influence upon the holders, to the remark that this event hushed the old slander about inferior natures in the negro, thence to the philosophy of slavery, and so through many detached thoughts to the end. It was nearly two hours long, but was very commanding. He looked genial and benevolent, as who should smilingly defy the world, the flesh, and the devil to ensnare him. The address will be published by the society; and he will probably write it more fully, and chisel it into fitter grace for the public criticism. He spoke of your unfortunate call, but said you bore the sulkiness very well. George Bradford was also very sorry; and it was bad that you should come so far, with the faces of friends for a hospitable city before you, and find a mirage only, or (begging Burrill's pardon) one house.

For the last six weeks I have been learning what hard work is. Afternoon leisure is now remembered with the holiday which Saturday brought to the school-boy. During the haying we have devoted all our time and faculty to the making of hay, leaving the body at night fit only to be devoted to sheets and pillows, and not to grave or even friendly epistolary intercourse. Oh friends! live upon faith, say I, as I pitch into bed with the ghosts of Sunday morning resolutions of letters tickling my sides or thumping my back, and then sink into dreams where every day seems a day in the valley of Ajalon, and innumerable Joshuas command the sun and moon to stay, and universal leisure spreads over the universe like a great wind. Then comes morning and wakefulness and boots and breakfast and scythes and heat and fatigue, and all my venerable Joshuas endeavor in vain to make oxen stand still, and I heartily wish them and I back in our valley ruling the heavens and not bending scythes over unseen hassocks which do sometimes bend the words of our mouths into shapes resembling oaths! those most crooked of all speech, but therefore best and fittest for the occasional crooks of life, particularly mowing. Yet I mow and sweat and get tired very heartily, for I want to drink this cup of farming to the bottom and taste not only the morning froth but the afternoon and evening strength of dregs and bitterness, if there be any. When haying is over, which event will take place on Saturday night of this week, fair weather being vouchsafed, I shall return to my moderation. Towards the latter part of the month I shall stray away towards Providence and Newport and sit down by the sea, and in it, too, probably. So I shall pass until harvest. Where the snows will fall upon me I cannot yet say.

Say to Charles that I was sorry not to have seen him; but if persons of consequence will travel without previous annunciation, they may chance to find even the humblest of their servants not at home. I know you will write when the time comes, so I say nothing but that I am your friend ever.

G. W. C.

XVII

CONCORD, *Sept.* 23, 1844.

Shall we not see you on the day of the cattle-show? Certainly Brook Farm will be represented; and I think you may, by this time, be farmer enough to enjoy the cattle and the ploughing. Besides, as I remember a similar excursion last year at which I assisted, the splendor of the early morning, which was not yet awake when we came away from the Farm, will amply repay any extraordinary effort. And still another besides; I do not want the winter to build its white, impenetrable walls between us before I have heard your voice once more. I should hope to come and look at you for one day, at least, in West Roxbury; but our Captain has work, autumnal work, the end whereof is not comprehended by the unassisted human vision. Potato-digging, apple-picking, thrashing, the gathering of innumerable seeds, must be done before winter; and yet to-day is like a despatch from December to announce that snow and ice and wind are to be just as cold this winter as they were the last.

And I have had a long vacation, too. I think, on the very day after I wrote my last letter to you, as I was whetting my scythe for the last swath of the season, my hat half fell off, and suddenly raising my hand to catch it, I thrust it against the scythe and cut my thumb just upon the joint. It has healed, but I shall never find it quite as agile as formerly. I could not use the hand—my right hand—for more than a fortnight. It was like losing a sense to lose its use. After a week of inaction in Concord, I went to Rhode Island and remained three weeks, and am now at home a fortnight. I came back more charmed than ever with Concord, which

hides under a quiet surface most precious scenes.
I suppose we see more deeply into the spirit of
a landscape where we have been happy. Then
we behold the summer bloom. It is spring or
autumn or winter to men generally.

We shall remain with Capt. Barrett through
the winter. The spring will bring its own arrangements, or rather the conclusion of those
which are formed during the winter. I suspect
that our affections, like our bodies, have been
transplanted to Massachusetts, and that our
lives will grow in the new soil. Not at all am-
bitious of settling and becoming a citizen, I am
very well content with the nomadic life until
obedience to the law of things shall plant me in
some home.

And are you still at home in the Farm?
Rumors, whose faces I cannot fairly see, pass by
me sometimes, breathing your name and others.
But I have long ago turned rumor out-of-doors
as an impostor and impertinent person, who
apes the manners and appearance of its betters.
I shall receive none as from you, however loudly
they may shout your name, except they show
your hand and seal.

Autumn has already begun to leave the traces
of her golden fingers upon the brakes, and occasionally upon some tall nut-trees. It seems
as if she were trying her skill before she comes
like a wind over the landscape. She warbles a

few glittering notes before the mournful, majestic Death-song.

Dear friend, why should I send you this chip of ore out of the mine of regard which is yours in my heart? Come and dig in it.

Your friend,

G. W. CURTIS.

XVIII

CONCORD, *January* 12, '45.

MY DEAR FRIEND, — I have written Burrill to look at the Custom-house, and inquire about the method of warming by water. He replies that he has been there, but defers writing to you until he learns more about the matter. Through him I received a message from Isaac to tell you that he (I) can procure an edition of the Beethoven Sonatas (26, I believe) for about $10.

I think it highly probable that I shall pass some weeks in Providence next month, and so will defer my day with you at Brook Farm until that time, of which I will inform you.

Burrill has not yet returned, and leaves me still a hermit. I am well pleased with my solitude, nor do I care much to go out of the country during the winter; but domestic circumstances make it advisable to go to Providence. There I shall have a good library at hand, which

JOHN S. DWIGHT

I miss a good deal here. Indeed, I think it
likely that every year while my home is in the
country I may perform a pilgrimage to the city
for two or three months for purposes of art and
literature and affection, for, as there seems in the
minds of divines to be some doubt of personal
identity when this mortal coil is shuffled off, I
am fain to embrace my friends' coils while they
are yet palpable. This idea of city visits implies
a very free life; but there seems now to be no
hinderance to it. When the band of Phalanxes,
proceeding into desert and free air, no more
allow art to rendezvous in cities, I can take one
of the nearest radiating railroads and rush from
my solitude into the healthily-peopled and city-
ish-countrified Phalanx.

I am loath to forgive Fourier the unmitigated
slander upon the moon. I began to suspect
that was the only influence alive since the sun
lights men to cheating and deviltry; and the
moon recalls the sweetest remembrance and best
hope. After our evening at Almira's it lighted
me home with such forgiving splendor that I
could have fallen on my knees in the snow and
have prayed its pardon if it would not have
chilled those members.

Almira I have not seen since Wednesday.
She was then well, and went with me to hear Dr.
Francis lecture upon Bishop Berkeley. He told
the life, which is the most poetical and beautiful

of any of his contemporary philosophers, and then suggested that the " limits of a lecture " did not permit an extended notice of his philosophy, and so gave none.

Among my holiday gifts was Miss Barrett's poems. She is a woman of vigorous thought, but not very poetical thought, and throwing herself into verse involuntarily becomes honied and ornate, so that her verse cloys. It is not natural, quite. Tennyson's world is purple, and all his thoughts. Therefore his poetry is so, and so naturally. Wordsworth lives in a clear atmosphere of thought, and his poetry is simple and natural, but no more than Tennyson's. Pardon these critical distinctions. I make them to have them expressed, for Burrill did not see why I called Miss Barrett purple. It was because her highly colored robe was not harmonious with her native style of thought. Ben Jonson, too, I have been reading. After him and Beaumont and Fletcher (who are imitators, rather, of Shakespeare), I feel that Shakespeare differed not in degree only but in kind from all others, his contemporaries and successors. In his peculiar path Jonson was unequalled, but Shakespeare includes that and so much more ! He seems to be the only one to whom poets are content to be inferior.

Remember me to Charles Dana and my other compeers at Brook Farm, especially Charles Newcomb. Yours sincerely, G. W. C.

XIX

MY DEAR FRIEND, — If I should come to Brook Farm on Thursday evening will it be convenient, and shall you be at home? If all circumstances favor, I should like to remain with you until Saturday. On Thursday I shall go into Boston to hear what the Texas Convention is saying, and if I hear anything very eloquent or interesting may not see you until Friday.

I was very sorry to know nothing of your convention until it was over. I should have run down to have seen you.

On Saturday evening I was at the Academy, and on Sunday at the Handel and Haydn. I have by Burrill a letter from Cranch, and a book of German songs from Isaac. More anon.

Your friend ever,

G. W. CURTIS.

CONCORD, *January 28th*, 1845.

XX

PROVIDENCE, *March 5th*, '45.

MY DEAR FRIEND, — I hope to see you at Brook Farm by Friday, intending to remain until Friday P.M. Here in Providence I have been having a quiet good time, though the weeks have

flown faster than I thought weeks could fly.
Mrs. Burges received a *Phalanx* from Miss Russell, in which we found a good deal of interesting matter. I hear from her that she will write by me to Miss Russell.

To-day it rains merrily, a warm southern April rain; and the weeks of mild weather hint that there must be ploughing and sowing very soon. I anticipate my summer work with a good deal of pleasure.

Yours truly and hastily,

G. W. CURTIS.

XXI

CONCORD, *March* 13, '45.

MY DEAR FRIEND,—The cold gray days at Brook Farm were the sunniest of the month. I wish I could step into the parlor when my heart is ready for music, and surrender to Beethoven and Mozart or, indeed, when I find men very selfish and mean, look in upon your kindliness and general sympathy. But while your intercourse at the Farm is so gentle and sweet you will not forget that it springs from the characters whose companions are still in outer darkness and civilization! I meet every day men of very tender characters under the roughest mien. Even in the midst of the world I constantly balance my ledger in favor of actual virtue, and enjoy intercourse, not so familiar but as sweet, as that I saw at Brook Farm. Is it not the tendency of a decided institution of reform to be unjust to the Barbarians? I do assure you the warm, tender south winds blow over us here in the unsocial state no less than the chilly east.

The snow on the ground belies the season. It is warm to-day and the birds sing. I should have enjoyed more my ride in the soft snow on Tuesday if conscience had not arrayed me against Mr. Billings. But I am most glad to see that I am withdrawing from the argumentative. I begin to enjoy more than ever the pure still characters which I meet. Intellect is not quite satisfying though so alluring. It is a scentless flower ; but there is a purer summer pleasure in the sweet-brier than the dahlia, though one would have each in his garden. It is because Shakespeare is not solely intellectual, but equally developed, that his fame is universal. The old philosophers, the sheer intellects, lack as much fitness to life as a man without a hand or an eye. And because life is interpreted by sentiment, the higher the flight of the intellect the colder and sadder is the man. Plato and Emerson are called poets, but if they were so their audience would be as wide as the world. Milton's fame is limited because he lacked a subtlety and delicacy corresponding with his healthiness and strength. Milton fused in Keats would have formed a greater than Shakespeare. If Milton's piety had been Catholic and not Puritanical I do not see why he should not have been a greater poet.

I shall not have much work to do before we undertake our garden plot. We take care of the cattle daily, and that is about all. Yesterday in the sunlight I walked in the woods. It was a spectacle finer than the sleet — the flower of winter among the trees.

I forgot to take the *Phalanxes*. Geo. Bradford asked me for a half-dozen. If you will send them to me I will give them to him. Almira says that he is now in a Brook Farm way. It is a species of chills and fever with him, as you know.

Remember me to the Eaglets, Dolly and her friend, Mary especially; and tell Abby Foord I have already learned the Polonaise which she is practising. I sit and play it over and over, and think I shall never tire of it. It has a peculiar charm to me, as I have never heard it except in the Eyrie parlor. It will always float me back to that room. Will you say to Charles Newcomb that Burrill has destroyed all "the churchmen"? Remember me to your family and believe me, as always,

G. W. C.

JOHN S. DWIGHT

XXII

CONCORD, *April 22d*, 1845.

Will you forgive me if I flood you with letters now while the mood of writing lasts? It seems that I must so exhaust some of the added life which spring infuses into my veins. The gray herbage of winter fades so slowly, so imperceptibly into the spring greenness, that I watch it with the curious eyes of a lover who sees gradual developments of deeper beauty in the face of his mistress. Do you note how every spring, sliding down from heaven with such intense life, quenches or rather subdues the remembrance of all past springs as a great gem surrounded in the ring by many small ones? And as I stood to-day, as if hearing the throb of the new active life in nature, for winter is more like the unchanged dead face of an intellectual person, the contrast of this steaming and heating life was suggested to me as is always the case, and necessarily so to the perfection of the thought. The idea of day is not symmetrical except when night is implied in thought, for if one could paint a portrait of the day, it would be brightness against darkness.

Why are we so troubled or moved at death, elated or depressed? It cannot give anything, nor take. Every sphere satisfies its desires by its hopes, and so seems to show that life is only an effort at equilibrium. At least it does show that to this state. There is a perpetual balance in every experience, never a permanence, as night follows day, but never survives the sunrise. Plato nor Shakespeare have drunk all this beauty, and it seems not right to become cold and callous towards it, externally, as the dead are. If they see the soul of things, do they see the form of nature without the soul, as we do now? If death mark only a general expansion of life and nature, it is no more pleasant. With greater hopes greater desires; and, after all, it is only keeping a larger set of books. There is no standard of life, as there is none of character. A flower is sometimes as pure a satisfaction as a man or the thought of an archangel. It passes into a proverb that the beggar is happier than a king, and proverbs are only the homely disguises in which wisdom roams the world.

The " Polarity " which Emerson talks about is the nearest approximation to the universal form of life, but this is constantly marred by a stray thought of permanence and the confusing hint of the passive mind that we suppose the balance to be the law, and are glad to accept night with day, and cold with heat, because there is a blindness in the spiritual eye which will not let us see the riper spirits who are not sated but satisfied with permanency. For there, too, is a reason that we are so glad to hide in the equipoise as an eternal fact that we are surfeited with constancy. Drowning in the malmsey-butt is no better than the Thames. Enjoyment to-day is secured by the certain prospect of sorrow to-morrow, which is not wilful, but a lesson of life, and as we suppose, at last, of the central life, just as the creation at daybreak is supported and adorned in the mind by the prospective tenderness of twilight. And this balancing, so universal in this sphere, in outward if not in real life, is therefore a fact, and why not as profound as any, since there is no standard of life? Is there any law at last? Nature seems so general and yet so intensely individual. As fine harmony results from the accord of distinct tones, and each tone an infinite division of vibrations. At bottom no things are similar. Harmony is only unison, not identity. Nature is like the ocean, which bears whole forests hewn into ships laden with treasure; but no bottom is found to support all the weight, only a drop resting upon a drop forever. The elephant that bore the earth stood upon a tortoise, who fortunately could keep his feet in his shell, and so had no need to stand anywhere!

The spring day looks very inscrutably upon all such wandering fancies. Her beauty is very inexorable, yet fascinating beyond resistance. It is not regal and composing and self-finding as is the mellowed summer, but an alluring splendor.

It is a bud in inner, as well as outer, expression, and not yet a satisfying flower. Yet in the young days of June is sometimes seen the sereneness of autumn. After the full summer it is quite plain. It is like a child with pale, consumptive hands. Yet this is a constant reference to unity, which just now seemed so far off. Beauty suggests what Truth only can answer and Goodness realize; and the whole circle of nature offers these three only, beauty, truth, and goodness, or, again, poetry, philosophy, religion, or, more' subtly, tone, color, feeling. This lies beyond words, because they are an intellectual means. Music foreshadows their interpretation, but always faintly, as it does everything, because music is revealed only enough here that we may not be surprised hereafter in some sphere. This is an intellectual sphere, but music is sentiment, so it is here an accomplishment for women, and for men of finer natures. Music is the science of spiritual form; and poetry, which is the loftiest expression of the intellectual sphere, finds its profound distinction from prose, which is the language of the vulgar, in its spiritual and sensuous rhythm, and so is music applied to the intellectual state.

Nature answers questions by removing us out of inquisitiveness. It is wilfully that we are querulous in nature, and not naturally.

I just now went to the door, and the still beauty of the moonlight night makes me a little ashamed of my letter. If I had stayed all day in the woods, and seen you there, I should have been content to be silent; but removed from the immediate glow of nature, and sitting in a purely human society, surrounded by circumstances produced humanly, as the house and furniture, the mind is withdrawn into a separate chamber, like one who goes down from the house-top into a room and so looks towards the north or west or south, and does not see all around as before.

Good-night, good friend.

Yr. aff.

G. W. C.

XXIII

CONCORD, *April 5th*, 1845.

Judge, my unitary friend, how grateful was your letter, perfumed with flowers and moonlight, to an unfortunate up to his ears in manure and dish-water! For no happier is my plight at this moment. I snatch a moment out of the week wherein the significance of that fearful word *business* has been revealed to me to send an echo, a reply to your good letter.

Since Monday we have been moving and manuring and fretting and fuming and rushing desperately up and down turnpikes with bundles and baskets, and have arrived at the end of the week barely in order. Yesterday, in the midst, while I was escorting a huge wagon of that invaluable farming wealth, I encountered Mrs. Pratt and family making their reappearance in civilization. All Brook Farm in the golden age seemed to be strapped to the rear of their wagon as baggage, for Mrs. Pratt was the first lady I saw at Brook Farm, where ladyhood blossomed so fairly. Ah! my minute is over, and I must leave you to lie in wait for another.

Evening. I have captured an evening instead, my first tolerably quiet evening in this new life, this new system of ours for a summer sojourn. The waves of my nomadic life drift me on strange shores, and sometimes, as I mount them, I dream of a home, quiet and beautiful, that home which allures all young minds and gradually fades into the sad features of such households as we see. In all my experience I think of three happy homes where the impression is uniform, for in all there are May Days and Thanksgivings; and yet to see a complete home would be to see that marriage which, if we may credit Miss Fuller, does not belong to an age when celibacy is the "great fact." As if the divine force could be extinguished! I must marry and spite her theory. You would be amused if you could see some of the letters which I receive, and which discourse of a wife with the same gravity as they do of washing clothes, as if each were a necessary, and that it would not do for me to settle upon a farm until I am married. There is some wisdom in the last advice. An old bachelor upon a farm, with a solitary old maid-servant, is not the most pleasing prospect for young one-and-twenty to contemplate. But I ignore farms and maids and prospects, saving always the natural one. Next year may find me the favored of all three.

How gladly I would be with you on Monday, you know; but what candidate for the plough and the broom should I be after the bewilderment of that scene! I remember too well the festivals which graced the younger days to trust myself within their sphere again, save in the midst of a boundless summer leisure. And when, after these chill, moist, April days, the perfect flower of summer shall bloom, I will be in its heart and breathe the enchanted air again. The word reminds me how glad I am that the flowers were so grateful. I committed my memory to delicate guardians, who, dying, did not suffer that to die. And the trinity of tone, color, and sentiment, though I knew not, like you, how to indicate it, is one of the most alluring of mysteries, so much so that I must leave it even unexpressed. Since so little may be known, I will not bring it into the melancholy purlieus of theory, but see it and hear it and feel it in echoes and glimpses. Yet all these rainbows which span the heaven of thought, finely woven of the tears of humility, one would sometimes grasp and crystallize forever. In that I find my satisfaction in what I know of Fourier; but to clutch at the rainbow! can it be crystallized?

Let not the spasm of infidelity mar my letter in your eyes or heart, and on your anniversary let one stream flow to the memory of your friend,

G. W. C.

XXIV

CONCORD, *April 17th*, 1845.

As a good friend, am I not bound to advise you how my new household works, here in the very bosom of terrible civilization, which yet keeps me very warm? A long wet day like this, when I have been gloriously imprisoned by dropping diamonds, tries well the power of my new solitary life to charm me. It has not failed. It is going away now through the dark, still midnight, but it bears the image of my smile. A long wet day, with my books and fire and Burrill for external, long thoughts for internal, company. After a morning service prolonged far beyond the hour of matins, led by the sweet and solemn Milton, I read Miss Martineau's last tale, founded upon the history of Toussaint L'Ouverture, in whom I have been interested. I have just read Victor Hugo's " Bug Jargal," his first novel, and also based upon the insurrection of St. Domingo. I feel that Miss Martineau's picture is highly colored, but the features must be correct. A strong, sad, long-suffering, far-seeing man, finally privately murdered by one who had been the idol of his manhood. The interest is individual throughout, which is necessary, yet fatal to the novel. I followed the Hero away from St. Domingo to his grave, and afterwards the thought of the remaining negroes came very faintly back. We read what Napoleon said of his own conduct in the matter; but with the abolitionist Miss Martineau on one side, and the doubtful Man of Destiny on the other, the pure fact grew very attenuated, and I am not now sure that I have seen it. The moment your curiosity is really aroused about an historical circumstance, the glasses through which you have been viewing so varied and wide a landscape become suddenly very opaque. History is a gallery of pictures so individually unexpressive that you must know the artist to know their meaning. Very few men relate with cold precision what occurs daily, so much are their feelings enlisted; and no less daily experiences are the recorded events of the past to the man whose days are devoted to them, and he too must infuse himself into them. He is a Guelph or a Ghibelline, not a judge of the struggle, wiser by five or six centuries of experience. In Carlyle's book " that shall be" the "Cromwell," I feel there will be so much stress laid upon the gravity and prompt, sturdy heroism of the man that much else will be shoved out of sight. It will be the history of Cromwell as a strong man, for Carlyle loves strong men; but if there are other things to be said, we shall not hear so much about them. So in Emerson's "Napoleon." He commences with saying that Napoleon is the Incarnate Democrat, the representative of the 19th century, and the lecture is an illustration of that position, but most comprehensive and eloquent.

Let history and great men fade from our sight. Lately I have grown to be a sad rhymer, and shall end my letter with hints of a life sweeter than these records of mine. More and more I feel that my wine of letters is poured by the poets, not handed as cold sherbet by the philosophers. Some day I may speak more fully upon these things. Meanwhile, secretly and constantly, I turn over pebble after pebble upon the shore, not uncheered by the hope that one day a pearl may glitter in my hands. Even this smacks of history, for Clio had claimed this page.

LADY JANE GREY

Meek violet of History! there flows
A modest fragrance from thy maiden fame
Touched with the coolness of the chaste repose
Which broods o'er Plato's name.

214

JOHN S. DWIGHT

No Wanderer through the dimly arched hall
Which Time has reared between thy date and ours
Meeting thy form, but sees that on its pall
    Are broidered Grecian flowers.

Thy shrinking virgin fame is wed with one
Whose calm celestial teaching was thy King;
When sitting in that cloistered nook alone
    Thou heardst the rude shout ring.

To thee that rabble shout foretold a scene
Of tearful splendor faded in its birth—
The melancholy mockery of a Queen—
    And virgin dust to earth.

Ah! Princess of that golden classic hoard,
Thy need was other than an earthly crown;
But ours was such, for else couldst thou have poured
    Through time thy pure renown?

For us thy blood was spilled; the whetted edge
Of that keen axe gave us one jewel more,
As a stream-drifted lily by chance sedge
    Is held beside the shore.

    Good-night. Let the remembrance of the
flowers still hold mine fast, and my solemn sweet
Milton shall sing my vespers too.

           May you "move
    In perfect Phalanx to the Dorian mood
    Of flutes and soft Recorders. . . ."

            Your aff.
             G. W. C.

XXV

CONCORD, *May* 3, '45.

I am weary of these winds, which have blown so constantly through the spring; and would so gladly exchange their long wail to-night for some of your music. And yet they are musical, and when I feel vexed at their persistency they seem to fade and breathe against my face with a low sigh, like one who shouts a secret which I cannot understand, and then mourns softly that I cannot. In spite of the wind we went to a new pond near us (new to us) this afternoon. There we separated, and Burrill went roaming over the hills and along the shore; and I sat down with Bettine upon the margin. That is the best work-book that I know. I read it for the first time in the Brook Farm pine-woods on a still Sunday; but to-day, as I followed her vanishing steps through Fairyland, the wind that rustled and raged around was like the tone of her nature interpreting to my heart, rather than to my mind, what I read. She was intellectual, spiritual more than poetical. She was such a glancing, dancing, joyous, triumphant child. I imagine great dark eyes, sparkling to the centre, and heavy locks overhanging — pine-trees drooping over diamonds, deepest brilliancy, with splendor, and a low singing sadness like the wind again, for her position is sad. The ardent, bursting, seeking-ripe girl, and the calm old man, wise and cold, not harsh. A sense of singular unfitness, a sweet-brier and an oak, a feeling as if some string in the great harp had slipped from its harmony, always strikes me when I read Bettine. Will you say no youthful lover would have inspired such a gush of the tenderest and profoundest girlishness? But it was no more than the bursting out of an irrepressible fountain, and it would have flowed as clearly and sweetly through a new wood conduit of to-day as through the polished golden channel which lay there for it. She must love, and love the best, and if only the best had been younger, fitter! Would not the steady massiveness of Goethe's nature have been splendidly adorned by the arabesques and intricately graceful woof of Bettine's? Now it was spring flowers on an old brow, with all the sweetness, but not the freshness, of youth. The imperial Goethe, supreme in wisdom and age, smelling a violet!. Ah! though the flowers and the laughter and the dance and the sparkle are for the child, but sadly serious autumnal wreaths for the old man; but the world does the best it knows how to do with the poets, so did Goethe with his young lover. Friendly, cool, gentle, never flattering, Bettine asks him half sadly, as if for once those world-roving eyes were still: Do I speak to you or only speak in your presence? She answered her question by asking it.

She speaks much of music. It is beauty impersonized to her; she pours out gems and flowers of words, and sketches grotesquely exquisite shapes dimly all over the landscape, coins all the beautiful fancies that crowd her brain, throws them to Goethe sparkling in the sunlight, and says: This is music, and finds at last that music is God. That is the most orthodox Pantheism.

The year has piloted us into the flowery haven of May, but I lay so languidly charmed with the beauty, and looking to see if I cannot this time see the goddess whose smiles I feel, that it will be June and summer before I know it. I treat the season as I do poetry. Sometimes I dissect a line which has fascinated me, or a poem, to expose the secret. But it folds and fades and changes under my glance as a cloud at twilight; and the beauty of the spring is as elusive as the foam upon a wave. In the midst of summer, the summer that we anticipated in January seems farther off. It sinks constantly into itself. The deep solitude of rest, the murmurous silence of woods at noon, these are as real in winter as when we are melting in June. The senses will have their share. It is melancholy that a man with the stomach-ache cannot enjoy Shakespeare; and that this wild, wayward, glowing, and glorious Bettine must disappear in the Frau von Arnim, wearing caps and taking snuff, and instead of these pine-trees, false curls, cut from the last crim-

inal, perhaps, and then croaking and child-bear-
ing and nursing and diapering! things so beautiful for many, but not for her. She is not yet a
woman, but belongs to us and the woods and the
waters and the midnight. A child singing wonderful songs in the starlight, serenading with
tender, passionate love-songs the old man who
waves his hand and breathes down a kiss which
is chilled by the night air, and falls like a snow-
flake into her hot bosom, not as a star upon her
brow.

We had some May-baskets left for us by
unknown hands upon May-day. The flowers
drooped over the sides, as if they would not
meet my eye to tell the secret; but a group of
smiling girls next morning were not so inexorable, and I thanked nature for such almoners of
her gifts. These beautiful tributes are touching
if one is serious. They are hung upon our wall,
which is adorned with the Urania and sketches
from Michel Angelo, and one or two drawings of
Burrill's.

Mrs. Brown (Mrs. Emerson's sister) wishes
Charles Newcomb to return some letters he has
about little Waldo's death. Will you speak to
him and say that Mrs. Brown will like them by
the first opportunity?

I hope my name is down as a subscriber to the
Paper. When shall we see it? Mr. Emerson
read us a part of your letter.

Here is another of the unconscionable epistles; not to mention answering, it is too audacious to demand that they shall be read.

Ever yr

G. W. C.

XXVI

Concord, *May* 31, '45, *Saturday morning.*

MY DEAR FRIEND,—Mr. Hosmer just tells me that he is going to Brook Farm, and I must say a word of regret that I could not come at this time, as Mr. Ripley, whom I saw in Boston, asked me to do. I have no doubt that the essence of all good things which are said, I shall gather from you some day, somehow. I send my subscription to the *Harbinger*. Almira is well, and would send you love and flowers if she knew that Mr. Hosmer was going.

I am fairly launched in " Consuelo," which I must read as fast as I can, for Mr. Hedge is to take it to Maine. Already it interests me as a new life, and, if I could, I would have it developing all summer; but I must feed upon the remembrance.

Will you say to Mr. Keith, the postmaster at West Roxbury, that we have despatched sundry messages to Messrs. Greeley and McElrath to have our *Tribune* come to Concord and not to

West Roxbury, and that to-day, upon receipt of his note, we have written a very concise letter upon that subject to the publishers.

Tell Mrs. Ripley that she must not fail to come this summer; and how soon are you coming to have a vacation in civilization?—not a day or two in winter, but a week for summer rambles.

Give my love to the Eyrie, for I believe all my friends are there save Miss Russell; and forgiving me for using you so unsparingly with messages, believe me always,

G. W. C.

If Geo. Wells is or shall be at Brook Farm, tell him that Almira and the rest of the Concordians are waiting to see him.

XXVII

CONCORD, *June 24th*, 1845.

MY DEAR FRIEND,—I finished "Consuelo" some time since, though I have not yet read the "Countess." I read what you said in the *Harbinger*, and am waiting for the promised continuation. Meanwhile you shall hear something of the impression she made upon me.

Consuelo is a natural, not a pious person. She

lives in the world like a flower, not like a flame; and though you feel that nothing is beyond her, since beauty and fidelity comprehend all, yet she does not directly suggest those personal relations with the Invisible which a saint always does. She sings as a bird, with her whole soul; and though she consents to relinquish the profession if she marries Albert, you feel very well that it will not be so. Porhora constantly urges the art upon her attention, but she grows in that by instinct. She is always in that to which he exhorts her, and the difference between her life and singing is no more perceived than in the life and singing of a bird. She is one of the persons from whom the rules of the art are drawn, because in her they are so clearly but unconsciously expressed. It is a character which fuses everything which it attracts to itself, and in whose outline no seam or crevice is visible. She is entirely impulsive, and every impulse is an inspiration. She leaves the castle of the Giants as soon as it occurs to her to do so, and the perfect submission to her impulse indicates the power and depth of her nature. Therefore, too, though she seems always right, she is free from all self-discipline. In meeting her one should not feel especially that she was a good person. She is not virtuous, for she has no moral struggle; not pious, for she is too impersonal; and even her love, at least to the end of "Consuelo," is not a life. Her regard

for Anzoleto you feel will pass. It is a personal
relation, necessary among the flowers and music
and moonlight of Venice. It is not the sentiment which love is to such a nature, nor could
Anzoleto ever awaken that. With Albert it is
much the same in another way. The waters do
not at once flow to a level. She is consolation to
him, but he is not life and hope to her. Music
is, but she is too human to be satisfied so. A
character like hers is always seeking for its completeness the strengthening sympathy of love,
although its relations are very far from personal.
Thus she seems as if she ought to love Albert,
and that she will at last. Her life is too self-
poised and true to allow you a moment's anx-
iety. The waves of circumstance roll and break
at her feet, and she walks queen-like over the
waters. The characters are grouped around her
as friends or courtiers; and so she preserves the
unity of the book as the figures of Jesus in the
old paintings. It is the memoirs of the court of
Queen Consuelo.

As in life such a person would make every
scene in which she was an actor impressive and
graceful, so the strong conception of the character makes the book so. I was thirsting for
music when I read it, and it satisfied me like a
strain of the sweetest and best; like a beautiful
picture or a flower, it left nothing to be asked,
although suggesting a general and not an indi-

vidual beauty and satisfaction like itself. The
graceful Venetian life wrought of song and fragrance fades so suddenly into the sombre Bo-
hemian forest where the careless girl who dabbles
in the water with Anzoleto becomes the mistress
of the destiny of the morbid Albert, and all shifts
again into the clear, vigorous friendship with
Hadyn and the sunny journey where the woman
of the castle becomes a girl again, as cheerful
but so much wiser than the Venetian girl, singing and saddening and sleeping in barns and leaping abbey walls, that it was like lying on a hill-
side under the shades and sunlight of the April
sky. There is an indirect developing of the
character throughout which is very fine as it
makes the harmonies more intricate and profound. It is like the reflection of the moon in
the water to one who has cast his eyes down
from the sky, as where Hadyn silently conquers
the love which she has inspired, because in her
mien and tone he reads her love for another.
That is a golden key to her character.

It was pleasant just after reading it to make a
trip to Wachusett with Mr. Hawthorne and Mr.
Bradford. We had soft, warm weather, and a
beautiful country to pass. From the mountain
the prospect was very grand. It is not too high
to make the landscape indistinct, but enough so
to throw the line of the level country on the east
back into the misty horizon and so leave a sea-

like impression. To the north was Monadnock, lonely and grim and cold. A solitary lover he seemed, of the rough Berserkir sort, of the round and virgin-delicate Wachusett. Towards the northwest the lower part of the Green mountain range built a misty wall beyond which we could not have seen had it been away. Nearer were smaller hills and ponds and woods. On the mountain we found the pink azalia and the white *Patenlila tridenta*. It was a fine episode in the summer.

About the 12th of July Burrill and I mean to go into Berkshire, and if possible to reach the White Mountains before the autumn catches us. This last is doubtful. But I felt when I came down from Wachusett as if I should love to go on from mountain to mountain until winter stopped me.

Last Sunday Father Taylor preached here. All the heretics went to church. In the evening he preached temperance. After the afternoon service we tea'd with him at Mr. Emerson's. He is a noble man, truly the Christian apostle of this time. It is impossible to pin him anywhere. He is like the horizon, wide around, but impossible to seize. I know no man who thrills so with life to the very tips, nor is there any one whose eloquence is so thrilling to me. I have found that one of the best things of living in Concord is that we have here the types of classes of men

P   225

and in society generally only the members of the class. The types are magnetic to each other and draw each into their vicinity.

The lonely life pleases as much as ever. If I sometimes say inwardly that such is not the natural state of man, I contrive to quiet myself by the assurance that such is the best state for bachelors. What disembodied comforter of Job suggests such things?

Yr friend,

G. W. C.

P. S. If you loved some one ardently who wonderfully resembled personally some one you hated ardently what would you do? It is not my case, but a question some evil genius whispered to make me perspire in these torrid days.

XXVIII

CONCORD, *Sept.* 14, 1845.

MY DEAR FRIEND,—I returned last week from a long and beautiful visit to the mountains, among which I had never been before. I went in the middle of July to Berkshire, and returned home for two or three days to set off for the White Hills, and back again through the length of Berkshire. In all about seven weeks. The garden served us very well. We had weeded so faithfully that weeds did not trouble us, and Burrill stayed in Concord a part of the time I was in New Hampshire.

When I first came towards the mountains it was twilight, and they looked very cold and grim; their outline traced against the sky, and seemingly made of some other material than earth or sky,—too dense for the one and too ethereal for the other. But when I came to them in broad day, they had lost their terror, as any other night phantom would have done. When I could scale them with my eye, and stand upon their highest peak, I seemed to have subdued them. But as I retreated, and looked back, they resumed their twilight majesty; and I could not realize I had been so proud among them. Yet, after all, they did not command me as the sea does. The charm of that is not robbed by being in it or upon it. All night and all day its murmur sounds an infinite bass to all that is done and said; and in the night, when you awake, it holds you still in thrall. Like the song of the locust in a summer noon, which fills the air with music and intensifies the heat, so the sound of the sea constantly draws thought and life to its depth and sweetness. Among the hills I was haunted with the vague desire of some corresponding sound. They were like a dumb Apollo, a thunderless Jupiter.

In Berkshire they are less grand than in New Hampshire, but high enough to cease to be hills, and wooded quite to the summit. They give an endless variety to the landscape, and are full everywhere of beautiful places and commanding prospects through the openings. The aspect of the country and the character of the people were so different from the country and people near a city, that it seemed to be more recently created.

Frank Farley is there in Stockbridge, and seems to be very happy. At Williamstown, the northern town in the county, we saw George Wells. He has only changed to become more entirely a collegian, but retains the same cordiality and carelessness that made us love him at Brook Farm. I have so many things to say about my wanderings that I cannot write any more, for I mean to come to Brook Farm and see you some day during the autumn. In the late autumn we are going to New York to pass the winter.

Give my love to Mrs. Ripley and the Archon, and to the two Charleses, and believe me, as always, your friend,

G. W. C.

On the next page I write a little song, which you shall print if you think it worth the space. Nameless and dateless if you please.

JOHN S. DWIGHT

Autumn Song

The gold corn in the field
  And the asters in the meadow,
And the heavy clouds that yield
  To the hills 'a crown of shadow,
Mark the ending of the Summer,
  And the Autumn coming in,
A crimson-eyed new-comer,
  Whose voice is cold and thin,
As he whispers to the flowers,
" Lo, all this time is ours."

I remember, long ago,
  When the soft June days were wasted,
That the Autumn and the snow
  In the after-heats were tasted;
For the sultry August weather
  Burned the freshness from the trees,
And the woods and I, together,
  Mourned the Winter, that must freeze
The silver singing streams
Which fed our Summer dreams.

Through the yellow afternoon
  Rolls the wagon harvest-laden,
And beneath the harvest moon
  At the husking sings the maiden;
While without the winds are flowing
  Like long aërial waves,
And their scythe-sharp breath is mowing
  The flowers upon the graves.
When the husking is all o'er
The maiden sings no more.

To ———

Thy spirit was a flexile harp, whereon
  The moonlight fell like delicatest air,
Thro' thee its beauty flowing into tone
  Which charmed the silence with a sound as rare.

Thou peaceful maid! the music then I heard,
  Whose influence had moulded thy soft eyes
To their deep tone of tenderness: O! bird,
  Whose life is fed with thine own melodies.

XXIX

CONCORD, *Oct.* 25, 1845.

MY DEAR FRIEND, — My Concord days are
numbered, but before I go I should like to write
you again, although it is not impossible that I
may come here again next year. The autumn
since I saw you has fulfilled the promise of the
day I left Brook Farm—bright, clear, and cool.
On Wednesday, the day was so remarkably beautiful that, having nothing especial to do, and
seeing that Ole Bull was to give another concert,
we walked to Boston and heard him once more,
I fear for the last time; and walked back again
the next morning. The air was very still and
bright, and cold enough to spur us on, without
an unpleasant chill.

I was very glad to part with Ole Bull having

my first impressions deepened and strengthened. The wonder with which I heard him in New York had subsided, and I gave myself, or rather he drew me, wholly to his music. It seems as if he improvised with the orchestra as a poet would at the piano. The music is full of every sort of movement and variety, but has great unity of character, and constantly suggests beautiful and distinct images rather than pictures. I thought of glorious young gladiators leaping into the lists, of fleecy clouds sweeping over starlight skies, and the beach-line of the sea. Every image was of the graceful, vigorous, and entirely healthy character of his person, which I suppose is only a fair expression of his soul. The music should not be criticised as a work of art, but only as the articulate reveries of Genius, for it is such as only he should play, because it is so entirely individual. It is full of delicate tenderness, and each piece is much like a gentle, strong child wandering in Fairyland, melted now by the sweets of child-deep piety in the Adagio Religioso, now leaping down the Polacca Guerricra like a young angel down a ladder from heaven, and roaming wistful and silent and amazed in the solitude of the Prairie, at times leaping and running and shouting, and then sighing and weeping and losing its voice in aërial cadences, until the smiles make rainbows through the tears again.

All these things whirled through my mind as I sat listening to him, with my eyes closed to preserve the realm of vision unassailed, last Saturday evening. But there is no end to such stuff. Music is so fully suggestive; and, after all, if you abandon yourself to that you are very apt to find yourself only among corresponding images. The adagio of the Fifth Symphony reminds me in one part of majestic waves, black and crowned with creamy foam; and they swell as if the whole sound of the ocean thundered in each, and when they have almost gained a height through which the sun may shine and reveal the long-haired mermaids, and the splendid colors which hide so much, then they fall upon themselves and stream backward into the sea, the foam uppermost like a shroud. But when I considered this one evening I found it was only the image of the sound transformed to a visible object. It is like watching the clouds and seeing their palaces and mountains. It is easy to sport with the symbol, and shows the greatness of the composer when he arouses the thought of the sea and sky for an echo; but that is only the sensuous influence of his music, and further we cannot go in words, for good music is so because it is inexpressible in words. There is always correspondence but not identity. And the impression of the same object in a poem, painting, or statue should be as different as the different necessities which constituted those arts and the differing direction of the various genius which so expresses itself.

Ole Bull's last concert (that I heard) was a cheap one, and the audience was very cheap. I felt at once the want of sympathy between that and him, and that destroyed the unity of the impression, which is so pleasant. The music which he played was of the best and played in the best way, but was played apart from the sympathy of the hearers to the soul of his art. When he was encored he came and showed his mastery of the violin as a juggler his power over cards. I should have been sorry to have seen it in any one but a true artist; but while he satisfied every just claim in the style and selection of the music of the concert, he permitted the rabble to hear what they had paid fifty cents to hear. He could not be accused of lowering or pampering the popular taste, for the music that he played was elevating, and the gymnastics not music at all.

I was glad to see Mrs. Ripley last Monday, and to hear from her the result of your Sunday meeting. I was a little sceptical, because I think permanent forms of worship spring from a very deep piety, and the pious persons whom I know I could count on my hands. Such themes are too good for heel-taps to a letter, and I shall wait the issue of your movement with a great deal of interest. Give my love to Mrs. Ripley, and tell her I hope the whole winter will not pass without my hearing from her.

I feel sorry to go from Concord, which we shall do in about a fortnight, for it is a quiet place, full of good people and pleasant spots. But I have found the same everywhere, so

"To-morrow to fresh woods and pastures new."

Your friend,

G. W. C.

XXX

NEW YORK, *December 22, 1845.*

A merry Christmas and happy New Year to you, if you are still alive, for since small-pox has joined your Phalanx I am not sure but his ambition for the supreme power has swept you all away. Yet every Saturday's *Harbinger* is a missive from Brook Farm which tells of other things than the cosmogonies, etc., of which it ostensibly discourses. I shall be glad to smuggle myself in for a share of the commendation bestowed upon those who have increased your list with the new volume, but my New York friends are pale at Greeley's *Tribune*, and would christen your sheet "An Omen Ill" instead of *Harbinger.*

Individually I am grateful for your article

upon De Meyer. It gives me an idea of his exhilarating impression, which I had dimly supposed from what I heard of him. I wait eagerly for his reappearance here, and cannot discover why he tarries so long in Boston. Privately I have heard very much good music since I have been here, mainly Mendelssohn and Spohr, with singing of Schubert and " Adelaide," etc. Publicly I have heard Huber, the German opera, and Mendelssohn's " St. Paul," a rich, melodious oratorio, squeezing the utmost drop from the power of the orchestra, and uniform at a point of the most luminous delicacy, refinement, and grace. I missed the heavy choruses of the Handel and Haydn, for, particularly, " Stone him to death," and " Lovely are the messengers," and " Oh, be gracious, ye Immortals " are magnificent. From what I have heard I prefer Mendelssohn to Spohr, as being the most original and luxuriant genius, although I hear that I shall not maintain that opinion when I have heard Spohr more.

Rossini and Donizetti are the Musical Gods here; now and then you meet a person who really loves what is better, but in mixed societies and at all concerts, particularly in fashionable circles, where music is a fashion now, the merest exercises for the voice and the fingers elicit the most rapturous bravoes and tapping of white gloves. Last evening I was at one of my musical friends', who, with another girl, plays the symphonies, etc., and is a most wonderful performer. She has the grand-piano which Miss Gserty (?) owned. For an hour we had the "Fingal's Cave," Schubert's "Wanderer" by Liszt, and Quatuors of Spohr; then entered "our fashionable friends" (for my musical lady is in such a sphere), and songs from Donizetti's operas and Thalberg's "Moses in Egypt," and the "Marche Maracaire," which seems nothing or very little without De Meyer, followed; and two mortal hours of such followed. I am always a little angry that my friends don't do something better on such occasions; but why cast pearls before swine? Yet I have no right to complain. They willingly play good music when they have good listeners.

Literature I serve quite faithfully. I have read the "Aminta," and am deep in " Hell." In German I am reading the second part of "Faust," with scraps from Novalis. English reading is Swedenborg and "Festus" and "Cromwell," with dips into the dramatists. I am sorry such good men have no better reader at this present, but trust they find some somewhere. The weather is vile. We are pinched with "nipping" airs which do not remain clear and steady, but unbend themselves in a dirty slush called snow in the papers. And just now I have no business to write you a letter, for I am torn every way by longings and doubts, not at all of a moral nature.

JOHN S. DWIGHT

This copy of verses, written last summer, is somewhat harmonious with my present mood, and
shall be printed if you approve.

I have seen Cranch several times, and his pictures. Some I like very much, but they have his
faults. I went with him to the Art Union Gallery the other day, and some beautiful landscapes
that I saw of his and others made my heart
"babble of green fields" to itself for some days
afterwards. One does not fully realize the value
of art until he is in the city, as away from home
you realize the worth of a mother's portrait. A
great charm of a picture-gallery is the perfect
stillness which belongs to the paintings, and
which they suggest. My overcoat seemed superfluous, for I was full of sultry noontide feeling,
gathered not from any special picture, but the
atmosphere of so many portraits of trees and
waters and hills.

In New York I feel how life is a glorious
opportunity wasted. A halo seems forever to
float over our heads everywhere, even on the
tips of the hair, which might crown us with glory
and honor; but no man is yet crowned. The
richest and grandest music of the world is hitherto in a minor key. But, indeed, every sigh is a
waste of so much energy that I try to turn my
stone towards the erection of the infinite temple
without grieving that it was not long since built.
I used to despise justice as a shabby virtue, but

now it seems to me the only lack.   We are unjust in our treatment and in our opinion of persons.   In the first we are too sweet, in the last
too severe.   For we eternally measure men by a
standard suggested by our individuality, instead
of sympathizing so fully that we stretch them
on their own line.   But here of all places there
can be no sham.   If we are not just in our own
thought we cannot pretend to be, since only
we are the persons concerned, and no man ever
cheated himself.

I should be very glad to hear from you, for,
knowing how busy you are, I have learned to
value your letters.   Remember me most kindly
to Mrs. Ripley, and believe me always

Yr friend,

G. W. C.

DIRGE

Time laid within an early grave
  Those hopes, so delicate and sweet,
I wondered not I could not save,
  But that they did sooner fleet.

Life has its fading summer dream,
  Its hope is crowned with one full hour,
And yet its best deservings seem
  Buds all unworthy such a flower.

How well that happy hour is bought
  By an after-life of sorrow!
The golden sunset yields a thought
  Which adorns the dreary morrow.

JOHN S. DWIGHT

We meet no more as we have met;
  Thy heart made music once with mine,
Which now is still, and we forget
  The art that made our youth divine.

One glance reaps beauty, nevermore
  It wears a lustre as at first;
We come again—the harvest o'er
  To no new flow'ring can be nursed.

XXXI

N. Y., *April 12th*, 1846.

MY DEAR FRIEND,—I meant to have given
you some verses when you were here as you
asked, but I forgot it. Now I send this. It is
so different from Wentworth Higginson's that I
do not feel as if the same road had been run
over by us.* And as each Phalanx will be a
centre of innumerable railroads in the age of
harmony, why not its paper of paper railroads
now? This was written in Concord some time
since.

Since you went I have done little but study
French and Italian. We meet Cranch, and his
wife of course, three times a week at that, and

* This refers to a poem by T. W. Higginson with the same
title, which had been printed in the *Harbinger* a few weeks
previously.

I drop into his studio now and then. To-day I was there, and he was hard at work upon a sunset composition, which he hopes to finish for the exhibition of the Boston Athenæum. He has sent the large landscape, "The Summer Shower," and "The Old Mill with the Bridge and Ducks," to the National Academy, which exhibition opens this week. He has sold one in Washington to a member of Congress for $100, and if he can continue to improve as rapidly as he has for a year or two past he will be a fine painter.

These soft, gushing spring days make me yearn for the country. I shall hope to be emancipated from Masters and Mistresses by the first or middle of May and take my place with the other cattle in the pastures. When I do not exactly know. Let me hear from you and about the Farm and its prospects. Burrill's eyes have given out again. He is bound head and foot, for his ankle has a habit of breaking down occasionally. Rest and warm weather and the country may strengthen them all. Give my love

"und vergiss nicht euer treur,"

G. W. C.

THE RAILROAD

A bright November day. The morning light
Shone through the city's mist against my eyes,
Soft, chiding them from sleep. Unfolding them
They raised their lids and gave me a new day.

JOHN S. DWIGHT

A day not freshly breaking on the fields,
And waking with a morning kiss the streams
That slept beneath the vapor, but on streets,
Piles of great majesty and human skill,
Stone veins where human passion swiftly runs.
Thereon I gazed with tenderness and awe,
Remembering the heavy debt I owed
To the dim arches of the dingy bricks,
Which sternly smiled upon my youngest years
And gravely greeted now, as through the crowd
By all unknown and knowing none, I passed.

The warning whistle thrilled the misty air,
And stately forth we rode into the morn,
Subduing airy distance silently;
The shadow glided by us on the grass,
The sole companion of our lonely speed,
And all the landscape changing as we went,
A shifting picture, of like hues and forms
But ever various, trees, rocks, and hills,
Rising sublime and stretching pastoral—
How like a noble countenance which shows
Endless expression and eternal charm.

I leaned against the window as we went,
And saw the city mist recede afar,
And lost the busy hum which haunts the mind
As a voice inarticulate, the tone
Of many men whose mouths speak distinct words
Which blend in grim confusion, till the sound
Like a vague aspiration climbs the sky.
The muffled murmur of the iron wheels,
And the sharp tinkle of the hurried bell,
And a few words between were all the sounds
Which peopled that else silent morning air.

A busy city darting o'er the plains
Across the turnpikes and through hawthorne lanes,
O'er wide morasses and profound ravines—
Through stately woods where red deer only run,
And grassy lawn and farmer's planted field—
Was that swift train that flashed along the hills,
And smoked through sloping valleys, and surprised
The mild-eyed milk-maid with her morning pail.

I dreamed my dreams until the village lay
White in the morning light, and holding up
Its modest steeples in the crystal air.
A moment, and the picture changed no more,
But wore a serious constancy and showed
Its bare-boughed trees immovable. I rose,
And stepping from the train, it glided on,
Sweeping around the hill; the whistle shrill
Rang through the stricken air. A moment more
It rolled along the iron out of sight.

XXXII

NEW YORK, *Thursday, May 14th,* 1846.

MY DEAR FRIEND,—You will of course have
supposed that I did not receive your letter of the
2d May, or it would have been more promptly
answered. On that very day I responded to a
most urgent invitation from Mrs. Cranch to go
up the river and make a visit with Burrill, at her
father's house upon the Hudson. I have only
returned to-day, and hasten to send you this,

bidding you to come, for the Choral Symphony is to be played, and there are to be various preparatory rehearsals of the orchestra and the chorus. This I know from the papers, but I will to-morrow inquire of Herr Timm the particulars of the concert. If I had not thought of remaining I would certainly do so if you will come. I am only sorry that there is no room fit for such a performance; it will be hard to get far enough away. Immediately that I have ascertained what particulars are ascertainable I will write again, although you must not wait for that, but come as soon as you can.

And now, what shall I say to you of the serene, sparkling splendors of the Spring which upon the Hudson have been flowing around me, so that my few days swelled into a fortnight almost, consecrated like a long song to romance and beauty. The tender young green upon the riversides and upon the mountains behind, which receive into their deep, dark mass of foliage the light, golden, smooth, colored fields which rise backward from the ample river, and (at Mr. Downing's at Newburg, opposite, a brother-in-law, and the author of fruit treatises, etc.) the splendid magnolias, which resemble deepest-dyed beakers, whence the fragrance arose almost palpable, it was so strong and sweet, and I looked to see rainbow-colored clouds floating from out the flowers—these, with the white blossoms of the orchards and the spray-like, snowy beauty of the Dogwood; in the early morning the sunlight, streaming down the mountains into the bosom of the river, kisses flashing and fiery, yet most gentle and tender, and at night the round moon, rising suddenly, almost without any preluding splendor over the same line of hills, and threw a yellow brightness all over the landscape like the throbbing heart of the night whose life is mysterious beauty fed by that mysterious light. What could I do but roam and wonder and smile and sing in the moonlight till midnight sent me to lie in a bed whence I looked out from under the plain white curtains through the branches of the trees without upon the sleeping river so wide and deep and still, and the line of hills fading in the night beyond. It was one of those seeds whose flower does not come at once, but which will show a tinge of Spring beauty wherever it unfolds. How have I earned the privilege of such enchantment, and is there not some condition of fairy which I do not yet see, but which some day must be paid?

The city is hot and hard after those fields and mountains, yet there are sweet smiles here, and I found three letters from friends, which was a fine welcome. Mrs. Dunlap and her sister are here, and I shall hear some singing, but they can give no music like the panorama I have seen. I have been choking all day, as I always do when I leave any place or person that is specially beautiful. When I am in the midst of the greatest beauty I remind myself that it is so, but I do not seem to touch the very heart; but when I have left it behind then its heart overflows itself in the remembrance, and so the past becomes more beautiful than any possible present, as when you would see a distant, almost indistinct, star you must look just at one side and not directly upon the object. The present must be as really worthy, but time and distance have a character of their own which they impart to all circumstances, as distance in space makes green and rugged mountains soft and purple like the hue of a fruit.

I long to leave the city, but I shall yet stay some time, for I shall not see my Father and Mother much during the Summer, and we shall sail probably by the first of August. Perhaps I can arrange so as to return with you if you come. I meant to have passed two or three days at Brook Farm. I could write till you were tired, but I have no time or paper. Cranch is well and sketching. He says something of coming to Boston during the Summer. Come immediately, and believe me as ever,

G. W. C.

XXXIII

NEW YORK, *Saturday, May* 16, '46.

MY DEAR FRIEND,—I learn from Mr. Timm that the concert will take place at the Castle Garden, a spacious enclosure adjoining the Battery. The Choral Symphony, the overtures to " Der Freischütz " and " The Midsummer-Night's Dream," Rico's singing, Burke's playing, and De Meyer's, if he is in town, will make up the bill. The rehearsals of the chorus and orchestra are separate until the night before (I believe); and the Symphony is found so difficult that they almost repent having undertaken it. I suppose there would be no difficulty in your getting to the rehearsals through some of your friends, as you did before. The orchestra is to consist of 150 and the chorus of 300 or 400 persons. " The Desert " is to be played for the fifth time on Monday evening. Trinity Church is to be consecrated on Thursday, the day after the concert, and Pico will doubtless sing somewhere during the week. I heard her and Julia Northall last evening in " The Messiah." Their voices were glorious. After the " Pastoral Symphony " the clear, rich, sunny voice of Miss Northall in the recitative " While Shepherds watched," etc., was most fitting and beautiful. It was a soft stream of pearly light, as the hope of Christ was upon

246

the darkness of his time. Pico sang, "I know that my Redeemer liveth," simply and sweetly, and was obliged to repeat it. The choruses were weak; they did not smite steadily upon the ear, but wavered, ghost-like, through the great tabernacle. The "Hallelujah" seemed to awaken the singers, and there was some tolerable body in that.

I heard Walker at his room with the greatest delight. He is so delicately feminine that I felt with him as with a splendid woman in whose nature you do not feel the want of masculine elements, since there is strength enough in a feminine way; with Rakemann I always feel the man with the womanly tenderness and sweetness which belongs to a real man. It was very pleasant to feel such a harmonious difference, as when you see a beautiful man and wife.

This being anniversary week, the Unitarians have been holding meetings and discussions. I do not feel impressed by them very much, they stand in such a negative position, "one stocking off and the other stocking on."

At Isaac's request I have been reading the life of the founder of his order, St. Alphonse of Liguori. He was a very pious man, and the Church was very jealous of him. It is a painful book to read, for the Catholic Church seems to use heaven as a weapon whereby to conquer the earth. I have not yet written Isaac, as he wanted me to read the book first; but if his promised prayers fall as short as the history, I shall be delivered incontinently to the buffetings of Satan.

I hope this will not find you at Brook Farm, for it cannot reach there until Monday; the concert is on Wednesday, if it is pleasant. Charles Newcomb and his mother are here.

Yours ever,

G. W. C.

XXXIV

CONCORD, *June* 6, 1846.

MY DEAR FRIEND,—I send you some verses for the *Harbinger*, which are not a conceit, although they relate to no actual personal experience except that I am sometimes conscious of the main fact, for my dreams do sometimes so surpass the waking reality that the charm of the suggesting person, if not lost, is indefinitely subdued and postponed. It is very pleasant here at Minot's. The family are still, the household goes smoothly on, and we live in a house 150 years old, under a tree of apparently almost equal age and looking across a green meadow to a clump of pines and birches beyond. The scenery in Concord is very gentle but pleasant. I have become attached to it as to a taciturn friend who has no splendid bursts of passion but wears always a soft smile.

All the morning we are busy working, and in the afternoons I have been reading Goethe's "Rome." It is very fine, and full of wisdom and beauty. His thoughts are clear and just and profound, and he looks on every side. He was so ready for Italy, too, as the home of art—he a lover and student of art, an artist by nature, and always too much a man. But Goethe, though he is constantly a wise friend, is never a lover. You could not take him always, personally, as the companion of your rambles, your jokes, your silence and sorrows. I think of several persons among those I know, who are by no means lights upon a hill, whom I should select as companions for a journey rather than him. In Rome one would wish to see him as he would Jupiter, and hear all his simple, grave, and catholic discourse; but has he that ineffable and inexplicable human delicacy and sympathy which is worth so much more in a man, as the innocence of the dove is than the wisdom of the serpent. And yet, in the "Elective Affinities," does he not show all that one could wish? But why should he be haunted by the thought that he does not have it and think of particular things to prove it, except that he does not have it? It is like feeling the beauty of single lines which a man writes without being impressed by the whole poem that he is a poet.

I had yesterday a long letter from Cranch and his wife. They are now in Washington, and are enjoying the same June weather that we have here. They have a peculiar interest to me as those who are to take the leap into the ocean whence we do not know whether we shall emerge upon some fairy island or upon desolate rocks or shall sink forever deeper and deeper in the sea-caves where the mermaids are. For a residence in Italy is certainly, in its entire uncertainty, in its new enclosures of circumstances and influences, like leaping into an unknown sea. It is a lover's leap, however, and love is beyond the hopes or arrangements of wisdom.

The Concordians are all well. I feel a pang in going to-night to take leave of Elizabeth Hoar, who is going away for several weeks, and who will not return until after I have left Concord. She seems to me one who may at any moment become invisible, like a pure flame. Almira is well, and sends love to you. She hopes you will come and make her a visit during the summer, and I hope it may be made in June, as I shall go away by the 1st of July, and move by slow stages towards New York. The summer will fly by on swift wings, and more beautiful than those of a gorgeous butterfly which we examined to-day; it flitted away among the dark pines, as the summer will disappear in the shadowy pines of autumn, so grave and at last solemn.

JOHN S. DWIGHT

I hope this late afternoon is as beautiful with you as it is here.

Your friend,

G. W. C.

DESTINY

That dream was life, but waking came,
  Dead silence after living speech,
Cold darkness after golden flame,
  And now in vain I seek to reach
In thought that radiant delight
Which girt me with a splendid night.

No art can bring again to me
  Thy figure's grace, lithe-limbed by sleep;
No echo drank the melody
  An after-festival to keep
With me, and memory from that place
Glides outward with averted face.

I loved thy beauty as a gleam
  Of a sweet soul by beauty nursed,
But the strange splendor of that dream
  All other loves and hopes has cursed—
One ray of the serenest star
Is dearer than all diamonds are.

Yet would I give my love of thee,
  If thus of thee I had not dreamed,
Nor known that in thine eyes might be
  What never on my waking gleamed,
For Night had then not swept away
The possibilities of Day.

251

For had my love of thee been less,
  Still of my life thou hadst been queen,
And that imperial loveliness
  Hinted by thee I had not seen;
Yet proudly shall that love expire
The spark of dawn in morning's fire.

How was it that we loved so well,
  From love's excess to such sweet woe,
Such bitter honey—for will swell
  Across my grief that visioned glow
Which steals the soul of grief away
As sunlight soothes a wintry day.

And so we part, who are to each
  The only one the earth can give,
How vainly words will strive to reach
  Why we together may not live,
When barely thought can learn to know
The depth of this sublimest woe.

XXXV

CONCORD, *June 29,* '46.

MY DEAR FRIEND,—I had hoped that you would have come to Concord yesterday, because to-morrow early I leave, and shall be here only one day more, towards the close of the next week. I had not expected to have gone so soon, but I shall accompany a sick friend to Saratoga by slow stages, and, returning to Worcester, make a short visit among my kindred there, and then return to Concord to take my final departure. I shall try to secure some day about that time to come to Brook Farm, if only to say farewell to you; but just now I cannot specify the day.

My trip to Monadnock was very beautiful. The minister, Jno. Brown, is the same Brook Farmer in a black coat; and I enjoyed a few days at his house exceedingly. I wrote a long journal while there, and cannot say anything about it here, therefore.

This afternoon I have answered Isaac's letter which I received during the winter. With great modesty I attempted to show him how, in the nature of things, proselyting was hopeless, at least upon any who are really worth converting. But the tone, like my feeling, was friendly and gentle. If it does not change his course towards me, he will better understand my feeling and position, for I told him that in men of his nature and tendency the zeal of proselytism is a part of the fervor of sentiment, and therefore I expected and willingly accepted his exhortations, and only deplored them as a loss of time and misuse of opportunities of communication. The Roman Church was such an unavoidable goal for Isaac that one who knows him well cannot possibly grieve to see him prostrate before the altar, and ought to understand and anticipate what was called his arrogance, which is a necessary portion of the sentiment and position.

The review of Mr. Hawthorne's book in the last *Harbinger* is delicately appreciative. The introductory chapter is one of the softest, clearest pictures I know in literature. His feeling is so deep, and so unexaggerated, that it is a profoundly subtle interpreter of life to him, and the pensiveness which throws such a mellow sombreness upon his imagination is only the pensiveness which is the shadow of extreme beauty There is no companion superior to him in genial sympathy with human feeling. He seems to me no less a successful man than Mr. Emerson, although at the opposite end of the village.

For a week or two, if you write, continue to address me at Concord, and believe me, in constant unitary feeling,

Your friend,

G. W. C.

XXXVI

CONCORD, *July 14th, '46, Sunday night*.

MY DEAR FRIEND,—I have just returned from Almira's, who sends her love, and will be very happy to see you. I have written Mr. Hawthorne to go to Monadnock with me this week, but I suppose his duties will prevent. If I go

I shall probably return before Sunday, as that is John Brown's working day, and we shall stay with him.

The night was glorious as I came from Almira's. The late summer twilight held the stars at bay; and in the meadows the fire-flies were flitting everywhere. Suddenly in the north, directly before me, began the flashings of the aurora—piles of splendor, a celestial colonnade to the invisible palace. It is a fitting close for a day so soft and beautiful. We took a long sauntering walk this morning and found the mountain laurel, which is very rare here.

I have been busy all my afternoons reading Roman history. Niebuhr and Arnold are fine historians. They are such wise, sincere men and scholars. I sit at the western door of the barn, looking across a meadow and rye-field to a group of pines beyond. My eye fixes upon some point in the landscape which constantly grows more beautiful, winning my eyes from the rest, until they gradually slide along, finding each as pleasant until the whole has a separate and individual beauty like a fall whose expressions you know intimately. It is a "Summer of Summers," as Lizzie Curzon writes me, and I am glad that my last hours in my own country will be so consecrated by beauty in my memory.

Burrill goes again to the Hudson to see Mr. Downing on Thursday. He will remain a week,

I suppose, and go again to New York in August, when I sail.

Let me have my answer in person, for so short and poor a letter does not deserve the exclusive attention of writing.

Remember me kindly to all at Brook Farm, to Wm. Channing particularly, if he is there.

Your friend ever,

G. W. C.

XXXVII

CONCORD, *July 13th*, 1846.

MY DEAR FRIEND,—It is a miserable piece of business to say my farewell to this blank sheet and send it to you, instead of having you say good-bye to my blank face. But, unless you can come to Ida's on Wednesday or Thursday, it must be so. A sudden trip to Saratoga has deranged my plans.

Will you now send my copy of the *Harbinger* to Almira?

We have been too happy together in times past and mean to be so so much more, here or somewhere, that we will not be very serious in our farewells, for we have been as far apart since I left you as we shall be when you are at Brook Farm and I at Palmyra. So good-bye, whether for two or three years, or an indefinite period.

When we see each other again we shall *meet*, for our friendship has been of a fine gold which the moth and rust of years cannot corrupt.

Will you give my love and say good-bye to Mr. and Mrs. Ripley and my other friends with you? and remember, as he deserves,

Your friend,

G. W. C.

XXXVIII

MILTON HILL, *Midnight, July* 16, '46.

MY DEAR FRIEND,—I could not come this evening, and shall only have time in the morning to go to Boston and take the cars; so we must part so. I will copy some of my verses for you if I can steal the time, and write you from Europe if David Jones permits me to arrive.

I must say good-bye and good-night in some lines of Burns's which haunt me at this time, though they have no appropriateness; but they have a speechless woe of farewell, like a wailing wind:

> "Had we never loved sae kindly,
> Had we never loved sae blindly,
> Never met or never parted,
> We had never been broken hearted."

Yr friend

G. W. C.

I shall write you again. Will you give this to Jno. Cheever? I have no wafer.

XXXIX

Fort Hamilton, Long Island, *July* 30, '46.

My dear Friend,—It is very shabby, but I have been so unexpectedly and constantly separated from my manuscripts that I cannot copy, as I hoped, some of my verses. I have but one more day on land, and more than I can well do in it.

Could you hear how the sea moans and roars in the moonlight at this moment, it would be a siren song to draw you far away. I strain my eyes over the water as one struggles to comprehend the end of life, but the beauty of the future lies unseen and untouched.

God bless you always, my dear Friend; and do not fail to write me often.

Affly. yr friend,

G. W. C.

XL

Rome, *November* 22d, 1846.

My dear Friend,—Italy is no fable, and the wonderful depth of purity in the air and blue in the sky constantly makes real all the hopes of our American imagination. Sometimes the sky is an intensely blue and distant

258

arch, and sometimes it melts in the sunlight
and lies pale and rare and delicate upon the
eye, so that one feels that he is breathing the
sky and moving in it. The memory of a week
is full of pictures of this atmospheric beauty. I
looked from a lofty balcony at the Vatican
upon broad gardens lustrously green with ever-
green and box and orange trees, in whose dusk
gleamed the large planets of golden fruit. Palms,
and the rich, rounding tuft of Italian pines, and
the solemn shafts of cypresses, stood beside
fountains which spouted rainbows into the air,
which was silver-clear and transparent, and on
which the outline of the landscape was drawn as
vividly as a flame against the sky at night. Beside me rose floating into the air the dome of
St. Peter's, which is not a nucleus of the city,
like the Duomo of Florence, but a crown more
majestic and imposing as the spectator is farther
removed. I had come to this balcony and its
realm of sunny silence through the proper palace
of the "Apollo" and the "Laocoon" and Raphael's
"Transfiguration" and "Stanze." The Vatican is
a wilderness of art and association, and in the al-
lotted three hours I could only wander through
the stately labyrinth and arrange the rooms, but
not their contents, in my mind, but could not escape the "Apollo," which stands alone in a small
cabinet opening upon a garden and fountain. It
was greater to me than the "Venus de Medici"

at Florence, although it has taught me better to appreciate that when I see it again. It is cold and pure and vast, the imagination of a man in the Divine Mind, given to marble because flesh was too recreant a material. The air of the statue is proudly commanding, with disdain that is not human, and a quiet consciousness of power. It does not resemble any figure we see of a man who has drawn a bow, but the ideal of a man in action. Like the "Venus," it shows how entire was the possible abstraction of the old Sculptors into a region of pure form as an expression of what was beyond human passion, with which color seems to correspond. Deities are properly the subject of sculpture because of color; colorless purity of marble accords with the divine superiority to human passion, and although the mythology degraded the gods into the sphere and influence of men, to the mind of the artist they would still sit upon unstained thrones.

This was one day. Upon another I stepped from a lovely road upon the Aventine into an old garden where, at the end of a long, lofty, and narrow alley of trimmed evergreens, stood the Dome of St. Peter's filling the vista against an afternoon sky. In these mossy and silent old places, the trees and plants seem to have sucked their vigor from the sun and soil of many long-gone centuries, and to remain ghosts of themselves and hoary reminiscences of their day in

the soft splendor of modern light. Italy itself
is that garden wherein everything hands you to
the past, and stands dim-eyed towards the future. It is a vast university, endowed by the past
with the choicest treasures of art, to which come
crowds from all nations, as lovers and dreamers
and students, who may be won to live among
relics so dear, but who mostly return to stand as
interpreters of the beauty they have seen. Therefore, Italy is a theme which cannot grow old, as
love and beauty cannot. Every book should be
a work of art, and Italy, like the Madonna,
should have a fresh beauty in the hands of every
new artist. It is no longer interesting, statisti-
cally, for the names and numbers have been told
often enough; but the impression which it leaves
upon the mind of men of character and taste is
the picture which should be novel and interesting.

But it is the relics of the summer prime of
the Rome of distant scholars and lovers, and the
art which shines with an Indian-summer soft-
ness in the autumn of its decay, that rule here
yet; for the imperial days have breathed a spirit
into the air which broods over the city still.
Although it is a modern capital, with noise and
dirt and smells and nobility and fashionable
drives, and walks and shops, and the red splendor
of lacquered cardinals, and the triple-crowned
Pope, in the arches which rise over modern

chapels and of which they are built, in the ruined forum and acqueducts and baths and walls, are the decayed features of what was once greatest in this world, and which rules it from its grave. My first view of old Rome was in the moonlight. We passed through the silent Forum, not on the level of the ancient city, which recoils from modern footsteps and goes downward towards the dust of those who made it famous, but by the ruined temples and columns whose rent seams were shaped anew into graceful perfection by the magical light, by the wilderness of the ruined Cæsar's palace, until we looked wonderingly into the intricacy of arch and corridor and column of which was built the arch-temple of Paganism, the Coliseum. The moonlight silvered the broad spaces of scornful silence as if Fate mused mournfully upon the work it must needs do. Grass and flowers in their luxuriant prime waved where the heads of Roman beauties nodded in theirs; and yet how true to the instincts of their nature were the Romans, who nourished by their recreations the stern will which had won the world for them. And since literature and art and science depend in a certain measure for their development and perfection upon a strong government, the same Roman beauty, in dooming to a bloody death before her eyes the man upon whose life depended other and far-away beauties and loves, may have breathed a sweeter strain into the song

262

of the poet. The Popes have not refrained from obtruding a cross and shrines upon this defence-less ruin. They would not render unto Cæsar the things which were his, and although they are shocking at first, the magnificence of silence and decay soon swallows them, and they appear no more except as emblems of modern Rome lost in the broad desolation of the imperial city.

'One cannot see the present Pope without a hope for Italy. I first saw him at high mass, with the cardinals, in the Palace chapel. The college of cardinals resembled a political and not a religious body, which, although the council of government, it ought to resemble upon religious occasions. When the Pope entered they kissed his hand through his mantle. He is a noble-looking man, of a dignified and graceful pres-ence, and already very dear to the people for what he has done and what he has promised. I could not look at him without sadness as a man sequestered in splendor and removed from the small sympathies in which lies the mass of human happiness. The service seemed a wor-ship of him, but no homage could recompense a man for what a Pope had lost. I have seen him often since, and his demeanor is always marked by the same air of lofty independence. It is good to see him appear equal to a position so solitary and so commanding, and to indicate this vigor of life and the conscience which would pre-

vent him from making his seclusion a bower for
his own ease.

From one of these wonderful days passed in
the Villa Borghese, a spacious estate near the
city, equally charming for its nature and art, I
went, a day or two since, to watch by the death-
bed of a young American. Hicks (a young
artist, whom I love and whom the MacDaniels
will know) and myself stood by him and closed
his eyes. He was without immediate friends,
except a connection by marriage who has recently arrived, and who was with him at the last.
I was glad that I was here to be with him and
lay him decently in his coffin. The handful of
Americans in Rome followed him last evening
at dusk, close by twilight, and buried him in the
Protestant graveyard, near the grave of Shelley's ashes and heart. The roses were in full
blossom, as Shelley says they used to be in midwinter. It is a green and sequestered spot
under the walls of old Rome, where the sunlight
lingers long, and where in the sweet society of
roses whose bloom does not wither, Shelley and
Keats sleep always a summer sleep. Fate is no
less delicate than stern, which has here united
them after such lives and deaths. And yet here
one feels also the grimness of the Fate which
strikes such lips into silence.

I force myself to send you this letter, because
I want to write you. It is a shadowy hint of

JOHN S. DWIGHT

what I think and feel, as all letters must be.
Cranch and his wife are with me, and will stay
the winter.   There are not many Americans, but
I look every day for Burrill.   Hicks I have seen
a good deal and like very much.   He speaks to
me of the MacDaniels.   Give my love to all at
Brook Farm, and forgive a letter which you will
not believe was written in Italy.   Cranch sends
much love.

Always yr

G. W. C.

How I wish you were going with us this sweet
sunny day (23 Nov.), on which I am writing this
at my open window, without a fire, to see the
"Gladiator" at the capitol.   It is a great respon-
sibility to be in Italy, one may justly demand so
much of you afterwards.   Once more, good-bye,
and some day send me a ray from the beautiful
past which Brook Farm is to me.

G. W. C.

XLI

NAPLES, *April 27th*, 1847.

MY DEAR FRIEND,—If it would be hopeless
and dispiriting to paint the constantly shifting
lights and beauties of a summer day, it is no
less so to write now and then a letter from Italy

265

to one who would so warmly enjoy all that I see and hear. Every omitted day makes the case worse, a month makes it hopeless; and so I lived in Rome for five months and wrote you only one letter at the beginning. Yet is the magnetism of friendship not yet fine enough for you to know how constantly you were remembered, how I lingered in the moonlit Coliseum, how I felt the commanding beauty of the "Apollo" thrill through me, and the "Laocoon" and the proud heads of Antinous, and the pictures which are what our imaginations demand for Raphael and Leonardo and Michel Angelo, how I stood in the flood of the "Miserere," which was and was not what I knew it must be, how I plucked roses from the graves of Shelley and Keats, and led a Roman life for a winter, not for myself only, but for you!

I have written quite regularly to my family, and described some of the many matters which were new and picturesque, but have scarcely snatched a line to a friend except to Lizzie Curson and two letters to Geo. Bradford, who had some intention of coming out to join us in this enchanted land. In my last letter to him, which I wrote at the end of the Holy Week, I mentioned the "Miserere" and the news of that time. He will show you the letter, I suppose, if you wish to see it. But from Rome I broke suddenly off and came to Naples.

JOHN S. DWIGHT

Is it not fine when things are beautifully different, when you part from one as if you were leaving everything, and find satisfaction in another—not a superiority, but equal difference? So is Naples after Rome. There is nothing solemn or grand in it. It rises in solid banks of cheerful houses from the spacious streets upon the water to the grim castle of St. Elmo, which hovers almost perpendicularly over it. These houses are white and bright, and turn themselves into the sunlight, and stretch in long lines around the bay, blending with the neighboring towns so that the base of Vesuvius is marked with a line of white houses, which go on undistinguishably from Naples. Farther round is Castellamare and Sorrento, whose promontory beyond is one corner of the bay, of which Capri seems like a portion sailed away into the sea. And the bay of Naples is so spacious and stately, so broad and deep, its lines those of mountains and the sea, its gem the sunny city, and the islands of Capri, Ischia, and Procida, so large and high and springing so proudly from the water, that it satisfies the expectation; and sometimes this broad water dashes and rolls like the ocean, then subsides into sunny ripples and gleams like glass in the moonlight. Two or three old castles stand out upon the bay from the city, picturesque objects for artists and lookers on, and in the hazy moonlight black and sharp masses reflected in the water. Sails and steamers and boats of all sorts are constantly dotting this space, and I am never weary of wandering along the shore on which lie the fishermen among their boats, with mournful looking women and black, matted-haired, gypsy-like children.

The picturesqueness of cities and life in Italy is more striking to me than anything else. The people are so poetic that, although lazy and dirty and mean, what they do and wear is like an animated picture. The gay costumes of the women —ribbons and bodices and trinkets—with their deep olive skins and bare heads, with hair that is most luxuriantly black, and beautifully twisted and folded in heavy, graceful braids, the broad-browed and outlined Roman women, majestic and handsome, not lovely or interesting, but showing as the remains of an imperial beauty; and in Naples the little figures and arch eyes and Oriental mien of the girls—these persons living in quaint old cities where the brightest flowers bloom amid hanging green over windows far and far above the street and walking in high-walled narrow lanes over which hang the sun-sucking leaves of the indolent aloe, and in which gleam the rich orange and lemon trees, or, as now, the keen lustrous green of just-budding fig-trees, and vines, or entering with quiet enthusiasm into festivals of saints, sprinkling the churches and streets with glossy, fragrant bay-leaves, hanging gar-

lands upon the altars while a troop of virgins, clad
in white and crowned, pass with lighted tapers to
the Bishop's feet for a blessing, or more grandly
drawing St. Peter's in fire upon the wild gloom of a
March night, and in vast procession of two or three
thousand marching down the narrow Corso singing a national song to the Pope—all this, if you
can unravel it, paints for the eye what can never
be seen at home. "I pack my trunk and wake
up in Naples," and find myself, for which I am
grateful; but I also find Italian beauty, which
is like American as oranges are like apples.
Such deep passionate eyes, such proud, queenly
motions, such groups of peasants and girls in
gardens listening to music, and lying asleep in
the shade of trees, all this material of poetry is
also material of life here. This is the true Lotos
Eaters' island, this the grateful land of leisure;
here people walk slowly and eat slowly and ride
slowly, and, I must say, think slowly. But that
also is corn to my mill. I find some sympathy
with the happy Guy of Emerson's book, for there
is no public opinion in Italy. A man feels that
he stands alone and enjoys all the joys and sorrows of that consciousness and that position.
Your room is your castle. If a man knows
where it is he comes to see you, but whatever
you do or say (of course excepting what is political) is your own business and not that of in-
fernal society, which at home is grand arbiter of

men's destinies. Except you care to do so, you have no state to keep up. The card for a royal ball finds you as readily in your fourth story as in the neighboring palace it finds My Lord; and so you are released from that thraldom which one cannot explain, but which one feels at home whether he consents to it or not.

And it is a broad and catholic teacher, this travelling. I have been quite unsphered since I have been here, in various ways, and have discovered how good every man's business is and how wide his horizon. There is a shabby Americanism which prowls proselyting through Europe, defying its spirit or its beauty or its difference to swerve it from what it calls its patriotism. Because America is contented and tolerably peaceful with a Republic, it prophesies that Europe shall see no happy days until all kings are prostrated; and belches that peculiar eloquence which prevails in small debating-clubs in retired villages at home. This is like taunting the bay of Naples with the bay of New York, or apples with oranges, or the dark lustrous beauty of Italian women with the blond fairness of Americans. Why should all men be governed alike rather than all look alike; the north is cold and the south is warm. These monarchies which are decried have been the fostering arms of genius and art; and in Italy and the rest of the countries here lie the grand achievements of all time, which draw the noblest and best from America to contemplate them and suck the heart of their beauty for the refining and adorning their own land. And why fear imitation! Men imitate when they stay at home more preposterously than when they see what is really beautiful and grand in other places; and a fine work of art repels imitation as the virgin beauty of a girl repels licentiousness. And we are elevated by art and mingling with men to know what is noble and best in attainment. We fancy a thousand things fine at home because we do not know how much finer the same may be, perhaps because we do not know that they are copies. Indeed, I feel as if it would be a good fruit of long travel to recover the knowledge of the fact which we so early lose—that we are born into the world with relations to men as men before we are citizens of a country with limited duties. A noble cosmopolitanism is the brightest jewel in a man's crown.

I have heard very little music in Italy—never so little in a winter. In Rome the opera was nothing, and there were only two or three concerts. That of a young Pole pianiste whom I knew was good, Maurice Strakosch (perhaps he will come to America). But the great gem of music was the singer Adelaide Kemble. You know she has left the stage and the public, but this was an amateur concert for the Irish. Her

singing of " Casta Diva " was by far the finest gem
heard. Such richness and volume, such possession and depth and passion, such purity and
firmness and ease, I did not believe possible. Although a single song in a concert it seemed to embrace the whole spirit of the opera. She sang also
the moon song from " Der Freischutz " simply
and exquisitely, also in a trio of Mozart's and a
Barcarolle, all of which showed the same genius.
I do not see that she lacks anything, for although
not beautiful, her face is flexible and really grand
when she is excited. Cranch thought her voice
not quite sweet in some parts. The " Miserere "
was exquisitely beautiful, but not entirely what
I expected to hear. In Naples I have heard the
" Barber of Seville " and an opera of Mercadanti's.
The last is refined street music, and reminds me
of the mien and manners of a gentleman. The
bands play every day, which is much better than
at Rome. But it is unhappy for me that Verdi
is the musical god of Italy at present, because
the bands play entirely from his operas, which
remind me of a diluted Donizetti. He has
brought out a new opera, "Macbeth," within the
month, at Florence. On the third evening he
was called out thirty-eight times; the young
men escorted him home in triumph, and the next
night various princes and nobles presented him
with a golden crown!

I have heard various rumors of Brook Farm,

none agreeable. I feel as if my letter might not find you there; but what can you be doing anywhere else? I have received no letter from you, no direct news from Brook Farm, except through Lizzie Curzon and Geo. Bradford. But it floats on in my mind, a sort of Flying Dutchman in these unknown seas of life and experience, full of an old beauty and melody. I know how your time is used, and am not surprised at any length of silence. We go into the beautiful country about us for a fortnight, to Salerno, Sorrento, Pestum, and Capri, afterwards Rome again. Florence, the Apennines, Venice, Milan, Como, the Tyrol, Switzerland, and Germany lie before us. What a spring which promises such a summer! You will still go with me as silently as before.

At this moment I raise my eyes to Vesuvius, which is opposite my window, and the blue bay beneath. I can see the line of the Mediterranean blending with the sky, and remember that you are at the other side. I write as if Brook Farm still was there, and am more than ever

Yr friend

G. W. C.

LETTERS OF LATER DATE

I

PROVIDENCE, *Thursday, Oct.* 10, '50.

MY DEAR DWIGHT,—I was very very sorry not to find you the other day ; but as I was only a few hours in Boston, I had no opportunity of renewing the attempt.

This morning I saw a letter, I suppose from you, in the *Tribune*, about Jenny's Saturday concert in Boston. It reminded me to send you a most rapid criticism(?) of mine published here yesterday. I address the paper as I do this note.

This Jenny Lind singing is a matter of such lofty art in the sublimest sense, and we are so young and jejune in all art, that I cannot much wonder at the general impression. It is precisely what would be the fate of really fine pictures and poems. Huge wonder, childish delight, intoxication, delirium, and disappointment—but little of the apprehensive perception of the presence of an artist so profound and grand.

I knew, of course, that you must be realizing

somewhere the greatness of this gift. Now I have heard you say so, I am glad to send you a kind of echo.

When shall I see you? I shall be here for a day or two more, then relapse into New York, for how long I know not. Let me have a line from you, saying that among all your virtues you yet count Memory, as does yours most remem-beringly,

GEORGE W. CURTIS.

II

PROVIDENCE, *March 17th, '51, Monday.*

I believe, dear John, that I have not yet had the grace to congratulate you upon " the great change " that you have recently undergone. But, happily, I am equally sure that you have not ascribed my silence to anything but the habit of epistolary silence that has come upon me since my return from the other continent, mainly distinguished, if my memory may confirm uni-versal remark, by the great number of letters written from it.

May I also add the satiety of writing, which a man who has just published a book may be sup-posed to be experiencing? For I *have* published a book, a copy of which, with the heart of the author, pressed but not *dried* between the blank

275

leaves, you should have had immediately but for my absence from New York. It is called "Nile Notes of a Howadji," and has thus far, being only a week old, received as flattering notice as any tremulous young author could have wished. One or two chapters are considered somewhat *broad*, I hear; but the whole impression is precisely what I wished.

I am here because I was invited to repeat my lecture here; and, as I was not back in New York when the "Notes" were issued, I preferred to tarry in the "ambrosial retirement," as Rev. Osgood calls it, and not serve as foot-notes to my Readers.

I shall go home soon, and I trust by way of Boston. If so, I shall of course see you and—yours, I must now say. Will you present my warmest regards and pleasantest recollections to your wife, and believe still in your friend

GEORGE W. C.

III

MY DEAR JOHN,—The Lady Emelyn swears by Venus and all the Goddesses that our party at your house must be postponed until Friday evening, that she may bring with us Miss Anna Loring and Miss Augusta King. What can mere men do? They submit. And they walk across the fields to look at a beautiful woman, at a Poet's wife.

We are all very hot and very happy down here, and wonder if your ashes are white or quite invisible, for of course, in the city, you have become ash.

Present us most kindly to your wife, and forget not that our coming will be much more enchanting with Mrs. S.'s proposed addition.

Yours aff.,

G. W. C.

NAHANT, *Wednesday morning Aug 12, '51.*

IV

MY DEAR JOHN,—We are tapering off. Mrs. Story is not well, and we have not our young ladies yet. Also C. P. Cranch goes to Quincy, where his wife is. So I fear you will have only William and me, and very probably his proof-sheets will retain him. I expect Cranch to come, but he is quite unwell.

Yours aff.,

G. W. C.

Friday, Aug. 15, '51.

V

PROVIDENCE, *Friday, Sep.* 26, 1851.

MY DEAR JOHN,—This morning I received the enclosed. If you can shed light upon the darkness it indicates will you please do so, sending me what information you have.

I am up to my ears in a book I am writing in continuation of the "Notes," "Syrian Sketches"; and shall stay here perhaps two months. I shall hope to slip down to Boston occasionally and see you all. I was there a few hours on Monday, and saw William by chance. Burrill has reached England, and is very much pleased with Malvern.

Give my love to your wife, whom I would be glad to hear sing once more.

Your aff.

G. W. C.

VI

PROVIDENCE, 25th Nov., '51.

MY DEAR JOHN,—I had intended to see the B. when she came. I have sounded her trumpet here, for auld lang syne. If I can do so heartily I will write a notice of her concert, as I always do when I am here, at the request of *The Journal*. I enclose my last effort in that kind, apropos of Catherine Hayes.

I would gladly come to Boston, but I cannot think of it just now. Should Jenny Lind threaten not to sing in Providence I shall very likely run down with my cousin Anna and hear her for an evening. We are trying to have the Germania

278

here, but for music in the general we go hang. My cousin, however, is a very accomplished player, and I enjoy with her Mendelssohn's songs and Liszt's arrangements and "Don Giovanni" and eke Schumann. I see Fred Rackemann has returned.

My book is written; but I am now very busily revising it. Hedge much prefers what I have read him to the other. He lives just across the street from me, and we have many a cigar and chat. He preaches superb sermons.

Give my heartiest love and remembrances to your wife, and forget not the faithful. I have a line from the Xest of Xtophers the other day, who is painting away for dear life. Tom Hicks, ditto. The latter lives with Charles Dana.

Ever your aff.

G. W. C.

I have unluckily forgotten your no. so I'll put the street, not being quite sure of that ! ! !

VII

TRIBUNE OFFICE, N. Y., 19th March, '52.

MY DEAR JOHN,—Your most welcome letter has been received, and its contents have been submitted to the astute deliberations of the editorial conclave. We are delighted at the prospect—but—we do not love the name. 1*st. Journal of Music* is too indefinite and commonplace. It will not be sufficiently distinguished from the *Musical Times* and the *Musical World*, being of the same general character.

2d. " Side-glances " is suspicious. It " smells " Transcendentalism, as the French say, and, of all things, any aspect of a clique is to be avoided.

That is the negative result of our deliberations; the positive is, that you should identify your name with the paper and called it *Dwight's Musical Journal*, and you might add, *sotto voce*, " a paper of Art and Literature."

Prepend : I shall be very glad to send you a sketch of our winter doings in music, especially as I love Steffanane, although she says, " I smoke, I chew, I snoof, I drink, I am altogether vicious." You shall have it Sunday morning, and I will address it to you simply at the P. O.

My book is ready, is only waiting for the English publisher to move ; and I have other irons heating, of which anon. I've had a long letter from Wm. Story, who is happy and busy in Rome—who wouldn't be ?

VIII

I wish you could run on and see us all. Tom Hicks is right busy with his great portrait of

the ex-Governor. Indeed, we are all so busy
that I have only time to remember—rarely to
say—that I am

Your ever aff.

G. W. C.

J. S. Dwight, Esq.

Give my kindest regards to your wife. I wish
she could sing in your paper.

IX

N. Y., *Saturday, 24th April, '52.*

MY DEAR JOHN,—I have been so busy in the
last throes of my "Syrian Howadji," which is to
be born on Tuesday, that I have not sent you an
intended letter about the Philharmonic and the
Quartette; and I presume from to-day's number
that you have other notes of them. I think,
however, I will still send you something by Monday's mail if you will promise not to use it if you
don't truly want it. There is rather a flat and
barrenness just now in the world of music, but,
with the Academy exhibition, Brackett's group,
and the Paul Delaroche picture we can make out
something.

Your paper is a triumph. It is so handsome
to the eye and sweet to the mind, it is so pleasantly varied, and its sketches have such completeness of grace in themselves, that the reader

is not ashamed of the pleasure it gives him and the interest he has in it, which you may have remarked is not always the case, for instance, in liking Anna Thillard's business at Niblo's (of which very little is certainly enough). I am half ashamed of myself for really enjoying what I know is so utterly artificial. Do you conceive?

I just see in the *National Era* a long notice of you and your *Journal*. It was not mine or the T.'s or I should have sent it to you. But you must find it.

You will receive an early copy of my Syrian book, the last of the Howadji, who, leaving the East, becomes a mere traveller. It was a real work of love, and I hope you may have some of the pleasure in reading that I had in writing it.

Give my love to your wife, and believe me always,

G. W. C.

I send you over the page a list of names of my subscribers and enclose you the funds in N. Y. money. [Enclosed were eight subscriptions to *Dwight's Journal of Music*, Curtis himself taking three copies.]

X

N. Y., 28*th Apr.*, 1852.

MY DEAR JOHN,—I span out my letter so far that I had no room for pictures, but I will

282

not forget them, and they will remain open until the middle of July.

I shall be only too delighted to see Mr. Gold-schmidt, and sincerely regret that I have enjoyed no such opportunity of seeing Jenny Lind until just as she is going. We are beginning to stir. White and I have both suggested *one* concert of the true stamp, and the *Times* came out against us and we pitched back again into the *Times;* and the *Herald* and other journals have called attention to the warfare, and insist that hum-bug, Barnumania, and high prices shall be put down. I am going to write an article upon Jenny Lind's right to ask $3 if she thinks fit, on the principle that Dickens, Horace Vernet, and every molasses merchant acts and properly acts.

Why not send your papers to the publisher of some Saturday paper to distribute with his? The difficulty is that if people are irregular in getting it, it will lose its character of steadiness, which is fatal to such a paper. Ripley agrees in this. By mail the majority of people who haven't boxes at the P. O. get nothing at all, or only spasmodically. You will have to send it to some agent here, I am confident.

Cranch is about breaking up house-keeping preparatory to his summer rustication. He is in a tight place again, as he is too apt to be, poor fellow! The fact is art is poor pay unless you are a great artist.   He fights very cheerfully, though, which is a comfort.   His children are very interesting, and at his house there is a set of us who have the best of times, the most truly genial and poetic.

I enclose you the funds which I so amusingly forgot, and, if I can serve you by seeing any agent or other "fallow deer," I shall be most happy to do it; and don't fail always to call upon me.

Yours most truly and ever,

G. W. C.

Is this sum right?

XI

NEWPORT, July 29th, 1852.

MY DEAR JOHN,—I have been running round for two or three weeks, and have forgotten to ask you to change the address of the papers which come to me. . . .

I am charmingly situated here with Mr. and Mrs. Longfellow and Tom Appleton, and with some other pleasant people.   It is very lovely and lazy; but I am quite busy.   Give my love to your wife and believe me, always,

Your aff.

G. W. C.

JOHN S. DWIGHT

XII

MY DEAR JOHN,—I leave Newport this evening, and since " friend after friend departs," you will hardly be surprised to hear that I have fallen from the ranks of bachelors; and that when I said I should die such, I had no idea I should live to be married. Prosaically, then, I am engaged to ... Her father is cousin of ... and is of the elder branch of the family, so that I already begin to feel sentimental about Lady Arabella Johnson. On the other side I come plump against plump old Gov. Stuyvesant of the New Netherlands. What with Dutch and Puritan blood, therefore, I shall be sufficiently sobered, you will fancy. Wrong, astutest of Johns, for my girl plays like a sunbeam over the dulness of that old pedigree, and is no whit more Dutch or Puritan than I am. She is, in brief, 22 years old, a very, very pronounced blonde, not handsome (to common eyes), graceful and winning, not accomplished nor talented nor fond of books, gay as a bird, bright as sunshine, and has that immortal youth, that perennial freshness and sweetness which is the secret of permanent happiness.

I am as happy as the day, and have no especial intention of marrying directly. Her father has a large property, but she is not, properly, a rich girl. I shall be settled at home in ten days. To-night I am going to Baltimore, and shall return to New York next week.

Give my warmest love to your wife, and believe me—Benedict or no Benedict—always

Your aff.

G. W. C.

XIII

N. Y., *14th April*, 1853.

CARO DON GIOVANNI,—Any time these six months I have seen a skulking scoundrel who endeavored to avoid my notice, and always turned pale when he saw a copy of *Dwight's Journal of Music*. I pursued him vigorously, and he confessed to me that he was the chief of sinners, and that his name was *Hafiz*.

"But," said he, when he saw in my eyes the firm resolve to acquaint the editor with the fact that his correspondent was still living—"but, oh! say that I have just paid to Messrs. Scharfenberg and Luis my subscription for the three copies owing the coming year"—and thereupon he vanished; and I haste to discharge my duty, for if I have a failing, it is doing my duty. Should you see the editor will you please state not only the fact of the subscription paid, but that I have heard this pursued Hafiz swear that not many moons should wane before he wrote to *Dwight's Journal of Music* a letter about things in New York, " our new music and other things," for instance.

Hafiz, who tries to make me believe that he does the music in *Putnam*, says that in the May number he has commended your *Journal*. He is an abandoned fellow.

How are you, and how prospers the *Journal?* and have you quite forgiven my wicked silences as well as my imperfect speeches; and will you please not to forget that you are never forgotten by   Your aff.

G. W. C.

XIV

N. Y., *Sept.* 14, '53.

My dear John, — I have just returned to town, and find your letter suggestive of White Mountains, quiet, artists, and other dissipations; but I am just from the hills, where I have been for six weeks, and am ordered to the sea-shore to be salted. I am not quite sure whether I shall go to Newport or to Long Branch; but I in-finitely prefer Newport, although I have very valued friends upon the New Jersey shore.

My old head has been bothering me all summer; but Dr. Gray has taken it fairly in hand, and says I shall soon be all right. I hope he is not all wrong.

I am coming to Boston some time during the season to lecture before your Mercantile Library, and have promised to make something of a visit; but I fear it will hardly be possible to stay long.

X was on my track yesterday, although I havn't seen him for an age. I hear he projects Europe again, but know nothing definite. To-day I am just hurrying off to Staten Island to assist at the nuptials of. . . . So they go, and so, soon—let us pray—may

Your aff.

G. W. C.

XV

N. Y., July 19, '53.

MY DEAR JOHN,—It has been anything but indifference that has prevented my sending you some notices of the pictures. But my head, which was muzzy when you were here, has been muzzier ever since, and my Dr. made me relinquish everything and run out of town, so that I have been gadding for a month, and the August *Putnam* hasn't a line of mine.

You see I have been positively idle; but I hope I am somewhat better. At least I feel so,

288

although I shall not work much for some time to come.

I'm going up to Cranch's this evening and to Lenox next week. It is not impossible that some happy gust may blow me to Conway. Give my kindest love to your wife, and believe me—muzzy or no muzzy—

Your aff.

G. W. C.

XVI

HOME, *9th Feb.*, '54.

MY DEAR JOHN,—Behold me with unspoken farewells and innumerable Boston banquets well (I hope) digested, and with only a glancing word with your wife at Mrs. Ticknor's on Monday morning.

One thing thou lackest, O Freunde! You have not heard Miss Skelton sing! It is a young girl who not only does not like " classical " music, but does not even profess to, which I hold to be virtuous in factitious times. But she is a sweet, natural, honest girl, and sings Italian, yea, even "Ah! Non Credea," with a sweet, full, and tender voice which is truly delicious. She is one of Cranch's stars. I heard her at the Greenwoods.

I have a vague idea of darting through Boston

again about the first of March. I shall be in New Bedford, and might go to Keene.

Good-night. I have every reason to love your Boston.

Your aff.

G. W. C.

Friday I hope to see Mrs. Downing, and if I hear of the great X—an unknown quantity to us—I will inform you.

XVII

N. Y., *Monday, April* 10, '54.

MY DEAR JOHN,— I send you my humble duty. The season is over, and I return to an accumulated mass of work. I find nothing pleasanter in my winter's reminiscences than the Boston episode.

Give my kindest love to your wife, and my regards to Hurlbut, and believe me as always,

G. W. C.

XVIII

WEST NEW BRIGHTON, STATEN ISLAND, N. Y.,
11 *April*, 1883.

MY DEAR JOHN, — Your letter reached me safely, and I share your surprise and regret at what seems to me, so far as I can see, a wholly unnecessary act. I will speak of it in the *Weekly* at once because the *Magazine* is always so long after!

I saw some notice of Cranch's seventieth birthday. Good lack! how the years whiz! I did not hear from him, and I suppose it is not exactly the occasion upon which you ask your friends to make merry. Longfellow, I remember, wrote me when he was seventy that it was like turning the slate over and beginning upon the other side.

We are all well and quiet. The Doctors in New York dine Dr. Holmes to-morrow, and I have promised to go. I have heard nothing from Edmund Tweedy for many a day, but I suppose that all goes well with him and his.

Good-bye. It is very good to hear from you always, and I am always affectionately yours,

GEORGE WILLIAM CURTIS.

XIX

WEST NEW BRIGHTON, STATEN ISLAND, N. Y.,
8 *February*, 1884.

MY DEAR JOHN,—I read your letter with sincere but hopeless interest, because I know how very slight her chance is in New York. The only hope lies in a circle of ladies who know her and would take pains to help her; but who are they, and how can they care for her? The contest single-armed against established teachers of prestige of a ci-devant Prima Donna, who had small success twenty-five years ago and is forgotten, is only pitiful. I will ask one of the best and most prosperous of our teachers, and who is much interested in my Lizzie, what ought to be done. He knows more than any one with whom I could advise.

I had heard with great delight of your portrait and of the becoming disposition which was made of it. I have thought also how sincerely you will deplore the death of our incomparable orator. And I hope that you sometimes think how affectionately I am always yours,

GEORGE WILLIAM CURTIS.

XX

NEW YORK, *October* 26, 1884.

MY DEAR JOHN,—Your note finds me here on my way to Ashfield. I voted for Edmunds every time, and in the uproar of the vote that made Blaine's nomination I held my peace. But had I voted for Blaine, and had afterwards found good reasons to change my mind, I should not have hesitated to take the course I have taken. I am very busy, and I send you my love always.

Your ancient,

GEORGE WILLIAM CURTIS.

JOHN S. DWIGHT

XXI

West New Brighton, Staten Island, N. Y.,
May 17th, 1886.

My dear John,—I do not know your address, but I am sure the Boston postmaster does, and I trust this note to his superior knowledge.

It was very good to see your familiar hand again and unchanged, and best of all to read your strong, clear, masterful, and delightful plea for the true saving grace of humanity, common-sense. It is a most admirable piece of work, and a host of readers will wonder that they had never thought of it before. That is the effect of all wise writing, I suppose, which like yours lays us all under obligation. Why don't you oftener bring us reports of your interviews with Egeria? Cranch had already told me of the paper with great praise, in a letter which told me also of your birthnight orgie with Boott and John Holmes. At the Commencement dinner of the year that Harvard made me a Doctor, I said to President Eliot, "Who is that military man who looks like a captain of Dragoons?" and, after making out the one I meant, he laughed and said, "Dragoons? why that is John Holmes!" As I remember him, his whiskers had a military cut; but I have often laughed since.

I have the photograph of Carrie Cranch's re-

markable portrait of you, which is a precious
possession; and when I see Cranch I hear of you
and when I don't see him I think of you, and
always with the old affection. We are all well,
which means my wife and daughter here, and
my son and daughter-in-law and two grandchil-
dren at Newton. My whiskers are white, but
my hair holds out with its old brown! Good-
bye and auf wiederschen.

Most truly yours,
GEORGE WILLIAM CURTIS.